Childlight

Childlight

How Children Reach Out to Their Parents from the Beyond

Donna Theisen
and
Dary Matera

New Horizon Press
Far Hills, New Jersey

New Horizon Press
P.O. Box 669
Far Hills, NJ 07931

Theisen, Donna and Dary Matera
        Childlight: How Children Reach Out to Their Parents from the Beyond

Cover Design: Norma Erler Rahn
Interior Design: Susan M. Sanderson

Library of Congress Control Number: 00-132564

ISBN: 0-88282-199-7
New Horizon Press

Manufactured in the U.S.A.

2005   2004   2003   2002   2001   /   5   4   3   2   1

Dedication

This book is dedicated to my beloved son, Michael Todd Owen, who died in a car accident January 3, 1998. Michael, thank you for choosing me to be your mother. Thank you for the love you brought to me and for the love I gave to you. Thank you for lighting up my heart and making it smile. You left me with a great void which I try to fill with that love. Your time with us was cut too short, but the joy you gave to us, your father, your sisters and myself, keeps us going until the day we see you again. And we will see you again. I love you son.

I'd also like to dedicate this book to all the mothers and their children who participated, and in doing so, allowed me to "hug my butterfly." Peace and love and think butterflies.

– Donna Theisen

Authors' Note

This book is based on the personal experiences of Donna Theisen and on extensive interviews and stories provided by parents and their family members who have lost children. In order to protect the privacy of a few individuals their real names and identifying characteristics have been changed. All the stories are true.

Table of Contents

Acknowledgments

Writing this book would not have been possible without the generous contributions of many people.

I thank all the mothers who shared the lives of their children with me and shared their pain, and mine, in telling their stories. The most difficult part of this project was the fact that all the participants became very special to me and their pain became my own. I am hoping that by participating in this project they will find some peace and healing. I pray that all of them come to know that they will see their children again in a better place. I pray that by giving others this glimpse of their children, their faith will be renewed. This is something that each of us lost sight of for a time. Our anger and pain were often directed at a higher power, along with anyone who played the remotest part in our children's deaths. This book has caused me to understand that each of us grieve in our own way, yet our grief is the same.

I want to thank Dary Matera for seeing the need for this book to be written and for his empathy and kindness to all the mothers. Thanks to our publisher, Joan Dunphy, for having the vision to realize that there are so many mothers and fathers out there who need to know that they are not alone.

A special thanks to Bonnie Blankenship of Hampton, Virginia for gathering her "M.O.M.s" and providing them with a special loop on the Internet that caters exclusively to grieving mothers. She and this virtual community saved my life and my sanity.

Also, thanks to a dear friend, Candi Fischer, for being there for me those first few weeks and giving me the support I needed to go on. To Debi, Marie, Nancy, Dianna, Beverly, Barbara, Ruth and Susie, thanks for the hugs and the laughs and the encouragement to live my life as Michael would have wanted.

– Donna Theisen

My sincerest thanks to all those who contributed stories to this book, especially to the dedicated members of M.O.M.s (Motivated On-line Moms).

Thanks to MN Susan for her crack research assistance and to publisher Joan Dunphy for seeing the light shining through the darkness.

– Dary Matera

Introduction

*"Perhaps they are not the stars, but rather openings in
Heaven, where the love of our lost ones pours through
and shines down upon us to let us know they are happy."*
— Eskimo legend

After the death of my son, I felt sad and alone. I began to
use the Internet to reach out to others across the world
for comfort and support. As I got more and more responses,
I discovered that those of us who have lost a child share
many common traits and experiences. Without question, we
feel it is the most horrible thing that has happened to us.
Losing spouses or parents is hard enough, but at least we
have the knowledge that they have lived long, full lives and
with them, we shared a rich past. Our children are our links
to the future. Our children had been parts of our bodies, lives
we shared on a daily basis from the moment they were born.
When our children die, it feels like parts of our souls are
ripped away forever.

For those who have suffered such losses, the pain
lasts a lifetime. We live with it every minute of every day. Our
priorities change. Our relationships change. Our entire exis-
tences change. It alters the dynamics of the rest of our families, consumes our thoughts and can tear apart our marriages. Friends treat us differently. They don't know how to
behave, so they often act clumsily, overcompensate and make
us feel worse. Some avoid mentioning the children's names,
not realizing that this often typical reaction greatly upsets

most mothers and fathers. Instead of tiptoeing around birthdays and anniversaries, we parents need to remember and sometimes even celebrate.

Male and female parents grieve in all the normal ways—and far beyond what most people would call normal. One day is filled with anger, the next denial, the day after debilitating guilt, the day after that a paralyzing sense of loss. It goes on and on until every painful emotion has been explored and repeated until we start inventing new ones.

We find ourselves doing crazy things to cope with the emptiness—whatever it takes to get us through the day. The courage needed to survive is tremendous.

At some point, almost all of us express anger toward God for taking our children. Some of us never get beyond this feeling. Parents who don't overcome their anger with God will often lose whatever religious foundation they previously had. This merely intensifies their misery. Even many of us who have made our peace with God deep down never fully accept what has happened.

All of us have had to develop individualized means of saving our sanity. These crutches, though oftentimes helpful in the beginning, can become both bizarre and harmful. They include everything from spiritualism to obsessions, drugs and alcohol—whatever gives comfort and eases the pain we do and we don't give a damn what anybody else thinks about our actions. We become very protective of our lost children's memories and overprotective of our remaining children.

Whatever our methods of grieving, we are a sad, psychologically damaged, but tightly bonded fraternity. There is an instant connection between two strangers who have both lost their children. Sometimes upon meeting or talking, we will hug and start sharing stories. We feel each other's anguish in ways no others can.

Clannish and wary of outsiders who don't understand our pain, we readily welcome each new member to our "roller coaster from hell" with hugs, tears and, most of all, complete understanding. And yet, in our own relationships, we are often intensely divided along gender lines. Husbands and wives usually deal with their grief in opposite ways, a psychological division that has the power to destroy all but the best of marriages. In many cases, men want to blot out their losses, rarely mentioning their children again. That's their way of healing. For them, to talk about their children is like jagged knives cutting through their hearts. In contrast, women often want and need to talk about their losses, often endlessly. For many women, it's silence that torments. Not surprisingly, a husband and wife can grow to fiercely resent one another for each person's insistence on acting in the precise manner that brings the other the most pain.

Even though we share the same anguish, the same losses, women mainly cling together while men mostly become islands of silence. Thankfully, I've discovered that I can phone any of my new female friends who've experienced similar losses night or day and they will drop everything and listen. I can cry, scream, yell, curse, get silly, make sick jokes and prattle on and no one complains. Although I've met only a few of them face to face, the love and acceptance we share is hard for outsiders to imagine.

Many of us mothers and fathers have come to believe that like the caterpillar turned into a butterfly, our children aren't gone, but are merely transformed. Our children are living in a world of light, freedom and joy. Until we have this belief to sustain us, we are the dead ones. Our lives are filled with pain, despair and hopelessness.

Our own transformation, from grieving individuals to people with hope, takes place when we come to believe very strongly that our children have remained with us in some form or another. We can communicate with them, feel their love and send our love in return.

These are our stories of how that transformation took place. I can only hope that in communicating the experiences we have had, others who grieve will find comfort and know they are not alone.

Chapter One

Donna's Story

One evening both my husband and son were out playing Evel Knievel on their snowmobiles. A call came in [to the 911 rescue center where I worked] for a snowmobile accident in that area. My heart stopped. Was it my own husband and son? I rushed to the scene. There were two sleds flipped over. A black-clad body was lying motionless between them. A trail of crimson blood extended from the body for sixty feet across the bright white snow.

In snowmobile suits, everyone looks alike. All snowmobiles look alike. Fear and dread gripped me as I approached. 'Please God, don't let this be someone I know,' I prayed. 'Please don't let this be a member of my family.'

My partner slowly removed the helmet from the person sprawled on the ground. I closed my eyes, then opened them. I breathed a huge sight of relief. It was a woman.

"Thank you, God," I whispered.

I immediately shifted into my medic mode. It may not have been my husband or son, but it was definitely somebody's daughter and maybe even somebody's wife or mother....

– Donna Theisen, Angels of Emergency

That harrowing incident happened nearly twenty years ago when my son, Michael, was a teenager and I was an Emergency Medical Technician. Although I was tremendously relieved, I never forgot the anguish I felt when I feared the accident had taken members of my own family. But even with that brief warning, I wasn't prepared for what occurred in early 1998.

For most of 1997, my second husband, Joe, was in the last stages of a losing battle with cancer. Joe's long illness had consumed my time and energy. Fortunately, I wasn't alone. Two years earlier, when Joe's cancer was first diagnosed, Michael, my only son and my youngest child who was then thirty-three, was kind enough to move from Ohio to Fort Myers, Florida to help me cope. I'd escaped the cold of Ohio ten years earlier following my divorce from Michael's father.

Michael was an outdoorsman who loved football, fishing, boats, water sports, playing pool and NASCAR. A mechanic by trade, I felt he was drinking too much and seemed to be wandering through life a bit lost. Still, he had an upbeat spirit and a good heart. Most of all, he was my only son. I cherished every moment we spent together. In this age of spread out families, it's wonderful when a parent can remain close to an adult child. As any mother can tell you, they are always our children no matter how old they are.

Joe died on September 21, 1997. Michael's presence and comfort were invaluable. I remember thinking over and over that I couldn't have survived this ordeal without him. Those thoughts proved to be a terrible omen.

On Saturday, January 3, 1998, at 8:00 A.M., I received a call from a social worker at the local hospital. He said they found my business card in the wallet of an accident victim and were trying to locate his family. The caller said the victim's name was Michael. "He hit a garbage truck head-on."

My heart began pounding. "Is he okay?"

I'll never forget what happened next. The social worker actually snickered. "He's not, really."

"I'm his mother," I said.

The man, realizing his faux pas, went silent. After finding out what hospital Michael had been taken to, I hung up, quickly got my things together and left the house. Jumping into my car, I sped to the hospital. When I got to the emergency room, a nurse directed me to the door of the trauma room where they had worked on Michael.

Walking into a brightly lit room and seeing one's child lying there covered in blood, lifeless eyes staring blankly ahead, is a horrible nightmare beyond words. It's an image that is seared in your mind forever, never to recede.

Knowing how little anyone in the hospital really cared about the passing of my son, I marched up to his body and began taking care of him myself. I closed his eyes, cleaned off the blood and brushed away the broken glass that was still sprinkled over him. I took the shark's tooth necklace he always wore from around his neck and put it on. My anguish was so intense, I wanted to die. I prayed to change places with him, for me to be on that table instead. I would have gladly given my life for his.

Later I learned that Michael had been at a party with his friends which lasted late into the previous night. In the early morning hours, he drove home, changed clothes, then dashed to his job at a boat repair shop. He arrived before the doors opened at 6:00 A.M., so he passed the time sitting in his black pick-up truck listening to the stereo. He must have realized he'd forgotten something important, because a few minutes later he cranked up the vehicle and took off for his home which was about six miles away. Like most people, Michael always used the same route. This morning, for whatever reason, he varied it by a few blocks. On the quiet, unfamiliar residential street, a huge garbage truck had stopped to collect some trash. The driver and workers saw Michael roaring toward them at approximately sixty-five miles per hour. Realizing something was wrong, the workers leapt from the vehicle. The huge garbage truck was hit so hard from the rear by Michael's small pick-up truck that it was knocked forward a foot and a half. The tremendous collision battered Michael's chest and head and trapped him inside the cab of his truck. The police had to use the jaws of life to free his body from the mangled wreckage. He went into cardiac arrest en route to the hospital and died shortly thereafter.

Those fortunate enough to have never lost a child have no concept of what I went through during the next few minutes, hours, days, months and years. The emotional pain was intense and relentless. They say it's worse for a mother who loses a young child, but I can't imagine how that can be true. In the days that followed his death, anything that reminded me of Michael made me burst into tears. I'd see a black pick-up truck and immediately start to cry. I tried to sleep late and put cotton in my ears so I wouldn't encounter or even hear a garbage truck—but there was no escape from the thundering machines. They seemed to be everywhere, day and night.

Sometimes I couldn't look at Michael's picture. Other times, I couldn't stop looking. When my husband Joe died, I had much different feelings. I could look at my husband's photos and remember him fondly, remembering our love and the good times. I've never been able to do that with mementos of my son.

During those first nights after his death, I slept in Michael's T-shirts and sweat pants and covered myself with his blanket in a desperate attempt to be close to him. I wore his jewelry for the same reason. I knew this was mentally unhealthy, but I couldn't stop myself. How much more could I take? I felt like I was dying a little each day. I longed to hug him and touch his face. I missed looking into his sparkling green eyes fringed with thick, black eyelashes. I missed the wonderful smile that lit up his face. I missed hearing his "rebel yell" as he burst through my door for a visit. I ached to see his little black truck parked in my driveway. I'd have traded an eye for just one more afternoon spent washing our vehicles together, spraying each other with a garden hose in the warm Florida sun.

I wanted to hear his silly jokes and study the changing contours of his face as he moved through the fourth decade of his life. I cried every Saturday night, remembering how we used to go to the auto races together and root for our favorite drivers. I wished I could laugh and taunt him again, because his drivers always lost. I even began to miss the things that used to annoy me about him. He always raided my refrigerator when he came over and it got so bad I tried to hide special treats I wanted to save for myself. Michael caught on quickly and soon learned all my hiding places. He seemed to take great pleasure in finding and devouring one of my sweet, hidden treasures. Whenever I would look for the treats later and discover them gone, I would rant and stomp my feet in anger, a chocolate craving left unsatiated. Now I would give anything to find the candy gone.

Michael was always charming nickel and dime loans out of me "till payday." I moaned, groaned and lectured him on fiscal responsibility, but I usually gave in. He also had a habit of "borrowing" all my favorite T-shirts and wouldn't return them unless I really got on his case. I groused and grumbled then lectured him on responsibility each time, all to no avail. Sadly, these "hassles" have transformed into some of my most endearing yet haunting memories. Given a second chance, I would gladly give him all the money and T-shirts he wanted.

As I endured those early days, while the small, every-day memories were deeply painful, the unanswered questions were even worse. Why did he return home that morning? Why did he take a different route, one he'd never used before? Why was he speeding on a quiet, suburban street? Unlike most young men, Michael rarely drove fast. His friends always teased him that he creaked along like a little old lady. Whatever the answers were to my probing and seeming end-less questions as to why this occurred, deep down I feared the accident was related to alcohol. He had been going to Alcoholics Anonymous for nearly a year, but frequently relapsed. Even so, he seemed enthused about the meetings and took comfort when he saw that other members who had struggled as he was struggling were succeeding. I should have been closer to him, helped more, seen his need, but I was blinded by my husband's illness and the constant care Joe required. I began to feel that I failed to give Michael the sup-port he needed and this guilt now ate at me.

I found myself wracked with guilt and self-loathing over all the lectures and scoldings I'd given him, over every-thing I ever had withheld and not freely offered for his plea-sure. Why didn't I cherish every moment I had with him? He was my only son, my darling boy. Why couldn't I have known in advance that his time here would be so short?

The guilt, pain and anguish continued to rip me apart to the point where I didn't think I could survive another day. Then something extraordinary began to happen that has for-ever changed my perspective on love, loss and death.

Michael's Contacts

Five days after Michael's accident, I pulled myself together and attended a support group meeting for grieving parents. I rose to my feet and told those gathered what I was feeling, focusing particularly on my anger and lack of understanding regarding the circumstances of the accident. The group was sympathetic and tried to offer support, but, of course, they couldn't give me any answers. They couldn't answer their own nagging questions, much less mine.

On the way home, I decided to pick up some things at the local department store. The route took me down a dark, rural road. As I drove, my mind was a million miles away. I was thinking about what I'd said at the meeting, thinking about how futile it all was. I told myself we were a bunch of messed-up saps pouring our hearts out—and what good did it do? No matter how much we sobbed and babbled, it wouldn't bring our children back. I began to cry out of anger and frustration. I loudly cursed God for taking my son from me. Then, all of a sudden, I saw a series a bright red lights blinking in front of me. I came out of my funk and slammed on the brakes. The car skidded to a stop less than six feet from the back of a tractor trailer that was parked on the shoulder of the narrow road. When the rush of adrenaline eased, I heard a clear, distinct voice inside my head: *This is what happened to your son. He never saw the truck. He was rushing home to get a tool he needed for work and was preoccupied.*

Somehow I knew I had been given one of the answers I had been praying for. I immediately apologized to God for cursing him. I thanked God for giving me the message and showing me what had happened in such a dramatic way. It was exactly the slap in the face I needed to bring me to my senses.

Enlightening as that experience was in giving me an answer to a torturous question I agonized over, it was merely one of a dozen tortures I'd erected in my mind. I quickly sank back into a deep depression.

A month after Michael's death, a friend took me to a gift shop that I had never been to before. She knew I was descending into darkness and wanted to try to take my mind off my misery. While browsing, I saw a display of shark tooth necklaces. My first impulse was to buy one for Michael. Then I remembered he wasn't around anymore. My hand instantly went to my throat, where I clutched the shark's tooth Michael was wearing the morning of his accident. I started to cry. Leaning on the counter for support, I took several deep breaths and tried to calm myself. Wanting to take my mind off the necklaces, I looked around and noticed a display of miniature doll house furniture. Sitting on a small hutch away from the rest of the display were two tiny cups touching each other. Each cup appeared to have some minuscule writing on its side. Curious, I wiped away my tears, picked up the first cup and squinted at the letters. It read "Michael." Startled, I put the cup down and brushed the writing off as a simple coincidence. *Michael is a common name,* I told myself. I stepped away, but something seemed to pull me back. I walked over to the display again and reached with my fingers for the second cup. Painted on its side was a pretty red heart and the words "I love you, Mom." A strange, warm feeling washed over me. The overwhelming despair lifted as I sensed that Michael was close. I felt better for the rest of the shopping excursion.

Afterward, when I returned home, I began doubting again. Was I merely finding what I so desperately wanted to see? Was I making mystical connections out of ordinary circumstances? I hadn't asked for a vision or message. I hadn't prayed for a contact with my dead child as some others do. I wasn't even certain I believed in such things. Basically, I was just wallowing in my own misery.

On the other hand, it defied the odds that those two cups would be displayed alone together on that hutch. When I had looked around in the shop, I saw that there were dozens of cups to choose from, all with different names. I both wanted to believe and didn't want to believe it was some kind of sign. I embraced the feeling of love and closeness the moment had provided, but I needed it to be real, not some disturbing side effect of my grief. Before I became a believer, other confirmation was needed.

I began looking for more strange occurrences, waiting, almost challenging Michael to show me that the incident with the cups was a real sign. For weeks nothing happened. My misery returned. I now grew more angry and resentful than ever. Fate was toying with my emotions. How dare it! Hadn't I suffered enough? I sank further into despair.

Late one morning, safe from the agonizing rumble of the garbage trucks I now perceived as demons, I was sitting in my dining room sipping coffee, contemplating the gloom of another long day. I stared aimlessly at a weeping bottle-brush tree I'd planted outside near the window in memory of Michael. *Planting the sapling is just another one of the silly things mothers do when they can't let go,* I told myself.

Suddenly, I was shaken from my dour daydream by some movement on the windowsill. I re-focused my eyes and was surprised to see an odd looking yellow butterfly that was flapping its wings furiously. The insect appeared to be trying to get my attention. When I leaned forward to observe it more closely, the butterfly waved its wings softly, then took off. I watched as the butterfly flew to the top of the bottle-brush tree, paused for a moment, then glided back to the windowsill. It turned toward me again and started to flap it's wings madly, then eased them into a slow flutter. The same warm feeling I'd felt in the gift shop swept over me. Tears began to spill from my eyes at that moment. I ached to reach out and hug my son. Suddenly, I heard a voice that seemed to be communicating with me telepathically. I immediately recognized my son's lighthearted, teasing tone. It was clear as the Florida morning sunshine. *Mom, how do you hug a butterfly?*

There was no mistake, no coincidence, no room for doubt this time. Michael had come back to comfort me and send me a message of love and hope. He was thanking me for remembering him and for planting the tree.

Later, I discovered that the butterfly is a symbol used by parent support groups worldwide to signify the rebirth of their lost children. In that insect's metamorphosis is a promise. A caterpillar crawls around a severely limited space, spins a cocoon, sleeps, then emerges as a splendid new life form that can float on the wind and soar above the trees, expanding its former horizons a thousandfold. This is what many parents feel has happened to their children; the children's spirits have transformed into new, more wondrous life forms.

My butterfly stayed for a while that morning, enjoying the sunlight with me, then drifted away. I wasn't sad to see it go, for I was sure it would be back.

The following week, I was meandering through the local Wal-Mart when my eye was drawn to a small, pink book sitting alone on one of the shelves. I wasn't even in the book section. Curious, I picked it up. The book's cover was totally blank, which was very strange. I opened it. The first page contained an inscription that leapt out at me: *To Mother With Love.* On the second page was written, "I am all the time talking about you and bragging to one person or another. I am like the Ancient Mariner who had a tale in his heart he must unfold to all. I am always buttonholing somebody and saying 'Someday you must meet my mother.'" The quotation was signed "Edna St. Vincent Millay."

Goose bumps rose all over my body. I read the words again. It didn't seem to be a poem and frankly, as such it wasn't very good. But the odd language was all Michael. He was always talking about "buttonholing" this person or that, or being "buttonholed" by someone else. He frequently told people they had to meet me, that I was "so neat." At the time of his death, he was working as a marine mechanic. He pronounced it "the best job I've ever had," because he loved being able to work on engines in and around the gulf. "I'm sticking with this one, Mom" he'd said at least a hundred times. "I'm going to be an Ancient Mariner!"

Naturally, I wanted to buy the book. I clutched it in my arms and immediately rushed to the cashier, fearful that someone would try and snatch it from me.

"I can't sell you this book," the cashier explained after looking at it thoroughly. "There's no price on it."

"Please, I have to have it," I begged. I stood my ground as the line grew behind me. The other customers began to grumble. The cashier paged the manager. The manager, a young woman Michael's age, finally arrived. She peered quizzically at the odd little book.

"There's no UPC bar code anywhere on it," she observed. "I don't even know how this got in stock. Sorry, Ma'am, but we can't sell anything without a UPC code."

I could feel the tears well up in my eyes. "Please, I need this book. It means a lot to me."

She hesitated for a moment, then searched again for the elusive UPC code. She found mention of the publisher, but no pricing information. "What the heck," she finally said. "Just take it," she offered with a shrug. I grabbed it like it was the Holy Grail and practically ran out of there before she changed her mind.

That night, I devoured the book cover to cover. It was indeed a strange little work that had no connecting story, point or obvious purpose. It simply read as if Michael was talking to me in disjointed bits and pieces. I felt a chill as I came to this line: "Guilt is causing you to think that if you had done something different, it would not have happened." After reading the words again, I heard my son's telepathic voice: *Mom, if I hadn't done what I did, you wouldn't be going through what you are now. I'm so sorry.*

This time, instead of being scared or feeling eerie, I simply answered out loud. "Michael, it's okay, baby. I understand you need to let the guilt go. We both do." As I spoke, I felt another burden release from my heart. I realized that I had been a good mother and there was nothing I could have done to better manage his life or to prevent the accident. As Michael had always told me, "That's my program."

After this, the contacts between Michael and me became less subtle and more startling. It was almost as if Michael was slowly drawing me into a new dimension, but didn't want me to be frightened. Now that I had come to finally accept the contacts as real, Michael was able to reach out to me further.

A week after the Wal-Mart incident, I was puttering around on the computer late at night when I noticed that Michael's digital alarm clock was facing the wall. He had brought it over to my house to make sure he wouldn't oversleep and miss work on those occasions when he spent the night. I couldn't recall having turned the clock around to face the wall, but I figured I must have done it to shield myself from further pain. My son used to sleep over so often I came to view the guest bedroom as his. It was almost like he was still a teenager living with me. Almost. Unwilling to completely cede over the space, it doubled as my computer room.

I turned back to the computer screen and scanned the Internet chat rooms and E-mail boards for information on grieving parents. I came across a particularly moving posting about a mother who, like me, was being contacted by her deceased child. It gave me such comfort to know that I wasn't alone. Tears began to flow down my cheeks. As I wept, I could see in my peripheral vision that a light was blinking somewhere in the room. Thank God I'd experienced the earlier contacts; otherwise what happened next would have terrified me. The digital alarm clock was now facing the room! The display was flashing 6:20 A.M., the exact time of Michael's death. My heart began pounding; my body tensed in fear. Not only was this surreal and otherworldly, but there didn't seem to be a comforting message behind it. The incident was stark, sudden and downright scary! Why was Michael or whomever, taunting me with that time?

I sprinted from the room and checked the other clocks and appliance timers for a similar, tell-tale flashing that would have indicated a brief power outage. Everything else was normal. Besides, I realized, if it had been a power failure, my computer would have turned off and Michael's clock would have been flashing 12:00, not 6:20.

I returned to the guest room, this time hoping that the "contact" was over. It wasn't. The clock still flashed 6:20. "You're scaring me, Michael," I said aloud. "Why are you doing this?" As the words left my lips, the clock went black as if it had been unplugged. I knew then he was just playing one of his dark and vexatious little jokes, jolting me the way he loved to when he was alive. "That's not funny, Michael," I scolded. "Things are a bit different now. Unless you want me to have another heart attack and join you, please cut this out!"

Despite my pleas, I could sense Michael was getting a big kick out of his macabre joke. True to form, the next three mornings I was awakened to the sound of him calling out "Mom, Mom!" Each time, when I looked at the clock by my bed, it was 6:20 A.M.

I told myself Michael was sure getting his money's worth out of this spooky gag. It wasn't until I was having my coffee on the third morning that I realized there was a method to his seemingly cruel madness. I had been painfully aware of the time of his death and was becoming almost obsessed with it. Whenever it was 6:00 A.M. or 6:00 P.M., I would freeze up and dread each second as the horrible moment approached. Regardless of whether it was digitally displayed on a VCR or microwave or pointed out by the hands on a standard clock or watch, 6:20 hit me like a sledge-hammer. I didn't want to see that time register, but I couldn't help this fixation on the time of his death. Michael obviously picked up on my dangerous obsession. As was his way, he wanted me to face it head on. He wanted to desensitize me to the time of his death by repeatedly flashing it in my face, forcing me to confront the inescapable fact that 6:20 comes twice a day, everyday. After the third morning, I never let that aspect of Michael's passing get to me again.

With that psychological obstacle cleared, Michael moved on to other areas. I was surfing around the Internet one evening when I received an "Instant Message" alert that someone wanted to "chat" with me. The message that evening was strange, because there was no user identification and the system I have is specifically set up to reveal the name of the person trying to make contact. Curiosity got the better of me and I decided to accept the invitation to chat.

The words, "I have a message for you," appeared. Still troubled by the lack of an identification, I typed back, "Who are you?"

"I am your angel."

Probably just a crackpot, I told myself, reaching for the disconnect key. For some reason, I stopped myself. I decided to play along. "Who is the message from?" I typed.

"Your son," was the response.

That got my attention. "Go ahead. I'm all eyes," I punched into my keyboard. Instead of the normal, sentence by sentence formation of the words, an entire paragraph of dialogue instantly appeared.

"Your son wants you to know that he is okay and happy, but he is worried about you. You are not smiling enough and you spend too much time alone. What happened to him was not your fault. It was his time to go. Your husband is with him and they are both worried about you. Michael wants to know why you quit writing and working on the book. You need to get back to the book. Michael says he loves you."

I was shocked by this mysterious Internet stranger who knew so much about me and Michael. I had a million questions to ask. I wanted more information. However, as quickly as he or she arrived, the Internet "angel" was gone.

As with the previous contact, this one frightened and troubled me. Mysterious messages through the computer? Was I completely losing my mind? That night I fell into a troubled sleep. I woke up with severe chest pains. I'd had two previous heart attacks, so I knew this wasn't good. I reached over to the night stand, fumbled for a nitroglycerin pill and put the pill under my tongue. This classic medication dilates the arteries and increases blood flow to the heart. However, instead of providing relief, I now began to feel worse. I took a second tablet. Still there was no relief. I started to panic, a stressful reaction that only served to intensify the problem. Pinned to the bed by fear and exhaustion, I was certain I was going to die. Almost instantaneously I heard Michael clearly say, "Mom, it's okay. I am not coming for you this morning. It's not your time yet."

Immediately, the pain subsided. I glanced at the clock. Not surprisingly, the display showed 6:20 A.M. Smiling, I drifted back to sleep.

The next few days I sat by my computer waiting for more messages from Michael or the "angel," but there was nothing. I listened intently for Michael's voice as I went to sleep or in the mornings when I first woke up, but still there was nothing. It was becoming painfully apparent that these contacts came at Michael's choosing, not mine.

Weeks later, after I'd all but given up hope of hearing from my son again, I switched on my computer one evening hoping some E-mail might provide a diversion. A few came in from various people, both real world friends and virtual E-pals. As I started reading the first E-mail, my Instant Message program beeped, indicating that someone wanted to chat. *Strange*, I thought. It was early evening, a time when I was rarely on the computer. I felt a familiar chill as I noticed that once again there was no identification given for the "caller." I logged on to chat with the mystery caller.

"Happy birthday," the first line read.

"Thank you, whoever you are," I typed back.

"Hope you have a nice one."

"Wait, who are you?" I asked.

"Mike."

That gave me pause. I collected myself and typed, "Where are you?"

"I am close to you," the response came back.

"May I confide in you?" I asked, feeling overwhelmed and happy for any company.

"I'm listening."

"My only son died in January. I was sitting here thinking about him. His name is Mike."

"I know."

"Is this a sign from him?"

"It may be."

"I believe it is," I responded. "I miss him so much. It's been a sad birthday until now."

"It is expected that you miss him."

"I sure do. He was my best buddy."

"He is aware that these messages ease your pain and he is happy about that. Do not fret. He wants you to be happy, so remember the good times and don't dwell on the sad times."

"I really try, but all night I have thought about nothing except the morning he died. I had to go to the Emergency Room...."

"He would not want that!"

For some reason, I turned away from the computer screen. The first thing I saw was Michael's clock. It read 6:20 P.M.

"Laugh and be happy," the unknown messenger advised. "That is what will make him happy."

"Are you an angel?" I asked.

"No. I'm no angel. Just be happy, Donna. That's what Michael wants."

The computer beeped, giving me a start. It took me a few moments to realize the sound was the routine signal indicating that one's chat partner has disconnected. "Mike" had vanished.

These contacts were becoming double-edged swords. I couldn't disagree with the fact that the bizarre encounters were helping me heal and that this strange, new, *Twilight Zone* world was a neat and often exciting place to hide. Still, reality continued to crash the party. A son who contacted me from the beyond every now and then was still no match for one who came over to visit me and was flesh and blood. I was reminded of his first message to me: *How do you hug a butterfly?* I couldn't help finding myself growing newly cynical and depressed. "My son, the butterfly," I spat out, ready to lose my way again. "How wonderful."

I walked out to the swimming pool to enjoy the sun before it set and try to head off my increasingly foul and bitter mood. I had just situated myself on a chaise lounge when I heard a delivery truck barreling down the street. The sound reminded me of the early morning garbage trucks. All the emotions bubbling below the surface sprang forth and I began weeping.

Laying there, looking straight up into the sky, the low hanging sun glistening off my tears, I was a miserable, self-pitying wreck. Slowly, my eyes began to focus. A huge bald eagle appeared out of nowhere. At first, I thought I was dreaming. I'd never seen a bald eagle before. Encountering the majestic bird in such an urban setting is extremely unusual. The giant creature swooped and soared around the house, obviously fixing it's attention on me. My son's voice popped into my head. *Don't like the butterfly, huh?* he teased. *Well, how's this?* The eagle swooped by again, so low I thought it would land on the roof. *I came as the butterfly so I could be close*, he then explained. *Mom, don't cry for me anymore*, he continued. *I'm free. I'm happy. Be at peace.* The eagle flew straight into the setting sun and disappeared.

I was both thrilled and depressed. The eagle was the most stunning physical appearance confirming Michael's ongoing existence yet. Who wouldn't want to be an eagle? If this was the afterlife—having the ability to become anything you wanted—then I knew Michael was indeed truly happy. On the other hand, Michael's message troubled me. It sounded like he was "crossing over" as the saying goes and leaving me forever.

"No," I pleaded. "Please, not yet. I'm not ready."

Michael must have heard me or sensed it himself, because the following week he returned. This time he came in a dream. I'm certainly no expert on paranormal phenomena, but it seemed logical to me that contact through dreams would be the easiest and most routine method. However, it's probably the least credible, as most people would write it off as "just a dream." That's why I was thankful Michael had chosen to appear in all the other ways first. That enabled me to accept the dream without question.

In the dream, Michael and I were walking side by side. We were laughing, talking and, best of all, touching. I could finally "hug my butterfly," and that made all the difference. However, the setting was strange and otherworldly. We were surrounded by a soft, yet very bright light, which seems like a contradiction, but that was my impression of it. I also recall that wherever we were, there were no floors or walls. I couldn't determine if we were indoors or out. It was mostly a place of light. After a while, Michael turned to me and gently said, "Mom, it's time to go." I could tell he meant that I had to go this time instead of him being the one to leave as before.

"I don't want to," I protested. "I like it here with you."

"You must," he countered. "This isn't your place."

I started to cry. The next thing I knew, I was back in my bed weeping. I glanced at the clock. As usual, it showed 6:20 A.M.

Later that morning, I recalled the various ways the contacts were made. It amazed me how Michael sometimes relied upon others to do the job for him. The "Internet angels," even the one named "Mike," appeared to be messengers rather than Michael himself. My logical mind wondered why this was necessary if they all had the same power and Michael could come to me himself. Maybe as in life, Michael wasn't computer savvy yet? Maybe being a free spirit who loves the outdoors, he had chosen a path in which his soul had become one with nature, not technology. Others may have preferred the reverse. This seemed logical to me. Yet, how could I be sure it was true?

One of my most recent contacts came in another dream. I was in a huge ballroom filled with large round tables. I was seated with friends and acquaintances. Michael walked over and took my hand. "Mom, you have to move from this table and sit over there by yourself." In previous contacts, Michael prodded me to get out more and not to spend so much time by myself, so I thought his command was peculiar. I asked him why he wanted me to move, but instead of answering, he just led me to a lonely table on the other side of the room. When we sat down, everybody else seemed to fade away. "Why do I have to sit here by myself?" I asked again.

"Because it will not be much longer now. I will be coming for you and you will be with me. You must prepare to leave all these people behind."

Yikes! I thought. *This is not the kind of message I want to receive.*

To those who suspect that these contacts with Michael were all based upon my own wishful thinking and delusions, I ask, why were so many of the contacts frightening and unpleasant? To me, the answer is obvious: they are real contacts, not tidy, warm and fuzzy self-created illusions.

In September, 2000, Michael's prediction almost came true. After having open heart surgery, during which there were complications, I stayed in intensive care longer than expected. I contracted pneumonia and had to be placed on a respirator. When that happened, I remember being in a place that seemed very strange. I was no longer in the hospital. The place I was in appeared to be somewhere between this life and the next one. My son was there with two young men I recognized as deceased sons of two of my friends. Michael was on my left. He kept saying, "Mom, you have to fight. Please, Mom, you have to fight." The other two men nodded in agreement. Mike continued, "It is not your time. You have things you still need to do." Even in this hazy state, Michael's words got through to me. I fought to come back, to get better. Mike kept saying, "You go, Mom." I know, without him urging me on, I would have given up. I would have joined him then and there.

I don't know what my timetable is or what time means to those who exist in the beyond, I just know that my time to leave this existence is drawing near. I will indeed be with my son again in the not too distant future.

I am ready.

Chapter Two

Sudden Losses,
Comforting Contacts

Each parent who has lost a child has a different story, yet the intense feelings evoked are all similar. And when the lost children communicate after death with their parents, the solace and comfort provided is immeasurable. Getting to that point, however, especially when a child's loss is sudden, as in an accident, can be difficult and even impossible. Ann Dawson, one grieving mother, tells of her experience.

Andy was the third of my four children. He had an inborn charisma. Although at times my son could be a little shy, he had the ability to light up a room with his presence and become the center of attention. When I look at photographs of Andy with his friends, he's always either in the middle of the picture or the other kids are looking towards him. I didn't realize how beloved he was until his accident. Even now, years after his death, his friends still visit his grave, leave mementos and cry when they talk about him. It's a tribute to him that he was so loved and has not been forgotten.

Andy was a football fanatic who played center on his high school team. His number was sixty-six. He named his wild and hyperactive Shetland sheepdog "Kelly," after his

favorite professional football player, former Buffalo Bills quar-
terback Jim Kelly.

Even though Andy was a football player, he didn't
shun students outside his circle like some young athletes do.
One of his best friends was a boy who suffered from an illness
that caused complete hair loss. Andy made him feel normal
and unashamed of his disease. My son used to rub his
friend's head good-naturedly for luck. It was a joke that made
them both laugh.

In July, 1997, Andy, his cousin and a friend drove to
visit Andy's older brother in college. The three young men
had planned to spend the night, but for some reason, they
changed their minds and started out for home at 4:00 A.M. It
was only a forty-five minute drive, so they figured they could
make it home despite the late hour. Forty minutes later—a few
miles from our house—the driver fell asleep and rolled the
vehicle. Andy was thrown from the car. My nephew was okay
enough to call his mother—my sister—from the scene and tell
her that Andy was hurt. My husband and I raced up the highway and arrived just as the paramedics were loading Andy
into the ambulance. He never regained consciousness and
died a week later on his father's birthday—July 27, 1997. He
was eighteen years old. Both of the other boys survived with
only minor injuries.

The following football season, Andy's teammates wore
his number, sixty-six, on their helmets during every game.

Before Andy's death, I hadn't been to a doctor in fourteen years except for yearly gynecology physicals and barely
ever took aspirin. In the days following his death, I was non-
functioning. My doctor gave me so many prescription drugs
to help me get through each day and night that I was in a constant zombie-like state. Eventually, I came out of my grief-
stricken haze enough to be able to begin setting small goals

for myself, like doing a load of laundry or making a meal for the family. After about a month or so of medication, I decided to wean myself from the sedatives and anti-anxiety pills, but I continued taking anti-depressants. I had not in my wildest imagination ever dreamed that the devastation of losing a child could be so overwhelming.

I had heard from others that Andy's death would change me forever and that scared me immensely. I liked my life and myself and I had no desire to change. As this meta-morphosis has progressed, however, I've become more com-fortable with the new me. I like my new self even better than the old. I have become much more spiritual. I've embraced a creative side of my personality that I'd buried for many years. I am a much more compassionate and selfless person. I get along better with my other three children now. I don't nag them and nitpick like I used to. My relationships with them are gentler, nicer. I value friends and family members more than ever before. I've often called these changes "gifts of bereavement." I realize that, as much as I hate it, Andy's dying has helped me become more of the person God intended me to be, even though I'm sure I still have a long way to go.

My husband and I have thrown ourselves into activities that we think might help others. All of the boys in the car had been drinking the night of Andy's death and Andy wasn't wearing a seatbelt. We've spoken to groups about seatbelt safety and the dangers of drinking and driving. Ironically, my husband owns a car dealership and before Andy's accident, had sponsored a program that was designed to encourage kids to buckle up. A few weeks after Andy's death, my hus-band filmed a commercial for the state police detailing how we lost our son because he was not wearing a seatbelt. The emotional public service ad showed pictures of Andy at his prom and graduation and included his father lamenting the fact that his own son had not heeded his advice. My daughter, Jill, Andy's girlfriend, two of his cousins and several friends have spoken to the students at Andy's high school regarding these issues as well.

Andy's Contacts

After Andy's death, I spent a lot of time alone and sunk into despair. My oldest two children had gone back to college, my youngest had started her second year in high school and my husband was away at work all day. I didn't reveal to any of them how badly I was actually doing, for I knew each of them was suffering deeply also.

One weekend about a month after Andy died, my grief was at its most intense and I came close to falling completely apart. I had this overwhelming need to know that my son still existed and was okay. I prayed to God all weekend for some concrete sign that would let me know my Andy was in heaven. Sunday was rainy and cloudy. I wandered around the backyard, staring at the gloomy sky. I sensed that if I received a sign, it would come from above.

By Monday morning, having gotten no messages or assurances from above, I was a basket case. I got out of bed and began shaking and crying. I stood in the middle of my bedroom, contemplating taking a tranquilizer of some kind to take away my pain. Just then the phone rang. It was my daughter, Jill. She was attending school at a university about three hours from home. I hadn't talked to her for several days, so she had no way of knowing how badly I had been doing all weekend.

It was about 10:30 A.M. and Jill's voice sounded as if she had just woken up. She said, "Mom, I have to tell you about the dream I had." When she said that, I was eager to hear it, because she'd previously had several very comforting dreams involving Andy, but I was also a little envious since I hadn't had a single one. Jill told me that she was awed by the vividness of this most recent dream. She had never had one so real. She said she could even feel a breeze blowing on her face. In her dream, she and I were standing in a field watching the sky as dark storm clouds gathered overhead. (Just like I'd been doing all weekend, unbeknownst to Jill.) I turned my back to her and the storm clouds parted. She saw intense colors that she had never seen before and stars that were aligned in the sky to spell out the message: "Hi, Mom, I'm home." Jill called out for me to turn around, but when I did, the sky turned dark and she suddenly woke up. She immediately reached for the phone and called me. She went on, "Mom, Andy's trying to tell you that he's right beside you; you're his favorite person, but he can't get through to you. You're not seeing these things."

When she told me this, I fell onto the bed and cried. It was, to me, the sign I was waiting for. I told her about my weekend and she said that if I had experienced the same dream I would have been skeptical, thinking it was my subconscious. Even now, years later, the message from that dream is my greatest source of comfort.

Jill was the conduit for a second, even more powerful contact. It was a little over a year after Andy's death and I was once again experiencing a depressed period. I missed Andy intensely. I wanted to be able to see him or talk to him and found myself praying for the ability to do that, even though I was sure such things can't happen. I drove to St. Charles, a quaint little town on the Mississippi River with lots of stores. It was a beautiful day and I decided to sit for a while at an outdoor café, have some lunch and read a book to get my mind off my sorrow. While there, my cell phone rang. It was Jill again. She was very excited. She'd just registered for the classes of her final semester. She was able to get all the courses she needed and was feeling very upbeat. We talked for a while about how great everything was going for her and then hung up.

A few hours later, as I was driving home, Jill called me again, this time in tears, sounding very agitated and upset. Through her tears, she said, "Mom, you won't believe what just happened to me." I thought her schedule might have gotten messed up, but I soon learned her distress had nothing to do with school. She explained, "I've just seen Andy." I began commiserating with her, telling her how I see kids that look like him all the time and how difficult it is. She interrupted me. "No, Mom, I saw Andy! I talked to him. I touched him. Have you ever heard of something like that happening?"

Then Jill told me the whole story: She had gone to a building on campus to drop off a homework assignment at one of her professor's offices. Walking through the hall, she saw a group of students coming towards her. All of a sudden, Andy stepped out of the crowd and called Jill's name. Jill had been so busy working out her new schedule that Andy hadn't been on her mind lately. Jill stopped dead in her tracks as Andy approached her. "It was as if my brain turned to jelly, as if everything around me froze." He was smiling his famous smile, wearing a raggedy T-shirt and had a ball cap on backwards. Andy touched Jill's arm and she began to shake. Then he said, "I've been looking for you. Are you going home much?" She shook her head no and he replied, "I'm going home a lot." She asked, "Where's home?" and he laughed and told her the name of our home town. She gave Andy her campus phone number and told him to call her if he ever needed anything.

The next thing Jill knew, she was walking alone across campus crying. She laughed and told me that if anyone had stopped and asked her what was wrong, she would have blurted out, "I just talked to my dead brother! Wouldn't you be crying?"

Later that same week, on Saturday night, I was alone in the house. My youngest daughter was spending the night with friends and my husband was out of town. My oldest son had asked to borrow some money for a trip into Chicago the next day and I said I'd leave it on the kitchen counter for him.

Late that night something woke me up. I wasn't frightened. I assumed it was my son stopping by to pick up the money. Just to be sure I called out, "Who's home?" and heard a voice downstairs say "Andy." My oldest son and Andy's voices sound identical so I assumed it was Andy's big brother as I had originally thought. As I fell back to sleep, I remember thinking what an unusual thing it was for my oldest son to call out Andy's name. He was devastated by Andy's death. He would not have been flippant about something like that. Still, there was no doubt in my mind that it was my oldest son who stopped by late that night.

In the morning, when I woke up, I went downstairs and was shocked to see the money I had left out for my son still sitting on the kitchen counter. I now believe it was Andy who visited that night to reassure me that he would be around when I needed him. The comfort I received from that contact with Andy was a great gift.

Shortly after Andy died, I had a dream that I had dismissed as wishful thinking. However, since then, I've come to believe it was more than that. In the dream, I was in a hospital waiting to see Andy. I knew Andy was dead. When Andy walked in the room dressed in a hospital gown, I hugged him. Then we sat down to talk. I asked him, "What's heaven like?"

It was his answer that made me dismiss the dream. He had replied, "It's alright. I've had a cold." Then he proceeded to show me that he was able to change shape and size. When I awoke, I thought that it wasn't a real dream visit, because I thought heaven had to be more than "alright" and I couldn't imagine anyone in heaven getting sick. Since then, however, I've read a lot about after death contacts and the afterlife and learned that sometimes, especially after a sudden death, there seems to be a "settling-in" period, often in a hospital-like location, for the souls to adjust to their new condition. I believe it's possible that Andy and I were together while Andy was still getting acclimated. Since then, I've become more receptive to the idea of dream visits. Because of my experiences and the stories that friends and family members have shared, I truly believe that Andy has a heavenly mission. He is to remind all of us that there is eternal life.

Our lives will never be the same without Andy. I doubt I will ever get over the grief, but I take comfort in all the wonderful contacts and reassurances our friends and family have received from my son reminding us of his continuing presence. I wonder how many other people have had similar experiences, but are too embarrassed to talk about these wonderful happenings. I truly believe our loved ones, in the first few weeks and months of their deaths, are eager to contact us and reassure us that they are okay and that they are still with us. I grieve for Andy every day, but I doubt that I would be a functioning human being without having received these contacts. They are undeniably gifts from God. The contacts are God's way of whispering in our ears, "He's okay. She's okay. I'm holding them in the palm of my hand. Don't worry about them."

– Ann Dawson

Another affecting experience of a young accident victim is the following one told by Deborah Callam who realizes that though her son is lost, his contacts are gifts of love and hope.

I was in the hospital with our baby, Walter. He was born prematurely and required a lot of medical attention in the beginning. When my husband came home from work, he began preparing dinner for himself and the other children. Suddenly, he noticed that our four-year-old son, Alex, and our two-year-old son, Robert, had disappeared. He looked around the house for them while our seven-year-old daughter, Elizabeth, checked outside. She brought Robert in quickly, having found him in the garage. She told her father she looked in the windows of the conversion van we had borrowed for a trip to Disneyworld, but didn't see Alex.

My husband sent Elizabeth upstairs to look for Alex while he checked the garage and the van again. When he opened the van doors, he found Alex pinned between an automatic reclining bench seat and a stationary bench. Somehow, the button that operated the movable seat (that folded down into a bed) had been pressed while Alex was in a vulnerable position. My husband ran inside and called 911.

The paramedics did all they could, but it was too late. Alex was pronounced dead at 6:52 P.M. on May 5, 1998. He died from mechanical asphyxia—suffocation. It wasn't until later that we discovered that the automatic reclining seats in that type of van can operate without the key being in the ignition.

The police speculated that Robert was the one who hit the button that moved the rear seat of the van that crushed Alex. There was no other explanation that made sense. Alex couldn't have done it himself. I think it's disturbing that something so dangerous can be operated by a two-year-old without the key being in the ignition.

My life has forever changed because of Alex's passing. I used to stroll through life without a worry. Now I realize that bad things can happen to good people. Caring for my other children, my days are filled to capacity, so I have little time to think. I prefer it that way. My nights are dreamless and most often sleepless. I was a mother of five before my thirtieth birthday and now I only have four children. When I dwell on that, life seems bleak. A positive side to all this is my relationship with God. I still love him and trust him a great deal. I pray more regularly than before and beg for peace. I am more accepting of people's quirks. I'm not in such a hurry. I try so hard to see the light through the darkness and reach out a helping hand to others in need. I watch sunsets, clouds, birds and all of nature with a great deal of respect for life, more than I had before I lost Alex.

Alex's Contacts

When my daughter Elizabeth went upstairs to search for Alex, evidently within minutes of his death, she said she heard his voice inside her head. Alex said, *I'm right here, silly. I am right here.* Elizabeth reported that his voice came from "up there," pointing to heaven. I believe that was Alex's way of comforting her and telling her that he would be okay in his new existence. Elizabeth has handled this so well, probably better than the rest of us. I believe it is because Alex came to her so quickly.

I went for a long time without any sign that Alex's spirit was still with us. I didn't even want to close my eyes, thinking that I might miss the sign when it came. Then one day I decided to stop looking and start feeling. I was no longer anxious about it, because I just knew Alex was still with us.

After I came to grips with this, things started happening. I was outside and a beautiful Monarch butterfly began flying around my head. It eventually landed on my shoulder. The butterfly stayed around our house for weeks and kept repeating the strange behavior. Pretty soon, I was able to mentally summon the butterfly whenever I wanted it to come around. What was especially compelling was the way the butterfly made little Robert laugh. I believe that was Alex's method of making sure Robert wouldn't carry any guilt with him in the future because of the accident.

My sister came over one day and we soon found ourselves outside. She was Alex's "special Aunt" and they had been very close. I told her about the butterfly, mentally called it and, sure enough, the beautiful insect appeared. "Wow, that's really neat, but it gives me the creeps!" my sister blurted out. The moment she said that, the butterfly flew away. Later, as she was getting ready to leave, my sister said, "I wish I could see Alex one more time." Instantly, the butterfly reappeared. She was overwhelmed with shock but I wasn't surprised at all. I thought, *Way to go, Alex! You've turned another person into a believer!*

Similarly, I was able to mentally connect with a deer that appeared in an opening behind my house. The deer always came alone. It never appeared with a herd as deer usually do. I'd just close my eyes and whisper "come to me" and the deer would materialize.

After these experiences, I began to be more interested in the spiritual aspects of life and death and began to examine them. Five months after Alex's death, my sister, my husband and I went to a spiritual workshop in Boston.

After four hours of intense spiritual activities, the class was given a restroom break. I was feeling really low, because the event was nearly over and I had not received a message from my son. Just minutes before, another woman had spoken with the spirit of her departed son and I was envious. I wanted it to be me. As I waited in line outside the women's lavatory, the dejection and disappointment became too much. I began to cry.

In front of me, two older women were discussing how moving the experience was between the mother and the son who contacted her during the session. That made me cry harder. They turned around and began consoling me. Although they were strangers, I openly poured out the details of Alex's death. I told them how I was at another hospital with my premature baby when the tragedy occurred, so I never had a chance to say goodbye.

It was soon my turn to use the restroom and we parted ways. When I came out of the stall, one of the women was waiting at the sink for me. "I am a medium and I have a message for you," she said. "Alex wants you to know that he understands how much you love and miss him. He says you are a great mother and he loves you very much, too. He also knows how hard you are working to get those vans recalled and he needs you to know that it is out of your hands. You must be patient and follow, not lead, on this. He said, 'Mom, you have always wanted to be in control. Even when Waltie was in the hospital, you had to know everything the doctors were doing and why. Now you need to have faith and trust that this will be done. You will save many lives, but you will never know it. I am proud of you and I love you very much.' That was the message from your son."

I was at a loss for words. I never told those women little Walter's name. And even if I had, Alex was the only one who called him "Waltie." This, to me, was concrete evidence that Alex had spoken to this lady. I stumbled out of the bathroom, searching for my husband and sister to tell them what the medium had said.

On Christmas Eve, 1999, I was alone looking out the window in my second floor bedroom, praying for strength and guidance. It had been a tough eighteen months since Alex's death and my life was becoming difficult to manage. Until that point, I'd had messages from Alex, butterflies and deer and sensed him around me, but I'd never actually seen him. Well, that was about to dramatically change. As I looked out the window, I saw Alex sitting high up on the branch of a tree, waving at me. Shocked, I stared at him, too afraid to move. Finally, I smiled back. But when I lifted my hand to wave at him, he was gone. In his place, at the exact spot where Alex had been, were two balloons—one red and the other green. The balloons had not been there before and they were very real. They didn't disappear like Alex. I looked carefully down at the ground around the tree. It had snowed the night before and there were no footprints anywhere near the tree. I know the red and green balloons were my Christmas present from Alex. Needless to say, that was a Christmas I'll never forget.

– Deborah Callam

Whether a child is very young, a teenager or an adult when they are taken, parents grieve for the baby they have lost.

Justin was our baby, the last of our five children. He was also the sole product of a "Yours, Mine and Ours" relationship. Our other children had come from previous marriages. When Justin was born on December 16, 1981, he cemented our family. He was "our" son and he was all the other children's real little brother. He gave us all something in common. Naturally, we spoiled him terribly.

It was so much fun having such a large family. Football season was a whirlwind. Justin played on his middle school team on Thursday, his brother played for the high school on Friday nights and his sister was a cheerleader for the local college on Saturdays. My husband, Kelly and I both coached baseball and softball as well. Like I said, it was a whirlwind.

I always thought of Justin as an "old soul." He was so curious about the world around him and was more mature than most teens. He seemed to have mentally outgrown his age. Don't get me wrong. He was a typical teenager in most ways, but he was such an individual. He walked his own path and was very particular about the people he let inside his world.

Justin had the most incredible blue eyes you'll ever see. They were enhanced by dark eyebrows and eyelashes. His hair was thick and became curlier as he entered his teens. He didn't like the curls, but I loved them and so did most girls. His girlfriend became part of the family. She is a wonderful, caring and compassionate young woman. Justin also had an unusual passion for being well-dressed—especially for a teenager. He didn't like shirts without collars and he owned only a few pairs of blue jeans. He saved his sneakers for athletics, preferring to wear slacks, button down shirts and dress shoes almost all the time.

Although he was only fifteen, he was already a towering six-foot-one. It amused him greatly that he was the tallest person in the family. He enjoyed football, but his favorite sport by far was baseball. He played first base and always made the all-star team in every league in which he participated.

As a young child, his nickname was "Pooh Bear," after the A.A. Milne character, Winnie the Pooh. When he got to middle school, he didn't want us to call him that anymore. However, in high school, he decided the nickname was cool and went back to it. He even bought a Winnie the Pooh tie to wear to his sophomore homecoming dance.

My favorite thing about Justin was his integrity. He had more character than any fifteen-year-old I have ever known. When a friend or family member told him something in confidence, that trust was never betrayed by Justin.

When our other children grew up and left the nest, we were able to spoil Justin even more. We were more financially secure and, on top of that, with four children living on their own, there was a lot less money spent on food. Justin tried to make up for it, however. Boy, could he eat. He was growing so fast it seemed like we could never keep him full. He was the sunshine of my days and the joy of my dreams at night. He was attentive to me and close to his father. They would spend many nights outside looking at the stars. Like his dad, he had a talent for taking things apart and putting them back together.

On August 20, 1997, Justin was riding in the flatbed back of a friend's pick-up truck when the driver pulled up next to a school bus filled with fellow students. The driver began talking with a friend on the bus and, without thinking, Justin stood up to do the same. When the driver finished his conversation, he took off, unaware that Justin was still standing up in the back of his truck. The sudden motion caused Justin to topple head first to the pavement and suffer extensive brain injuries. The next twenty hours were pure hell. We stayed with him the whole time. His body was warm and his heart was beating strongly, but his brain was dead. He couldn't breathe on his own. The machines and medicines were all that were keeping his body alive. The next day, the doctors made it official. He was pronounced dead.

Afterward, time seemed to pass in a blur. I can't believe I survived that first year without my "Pooh Bear." Sometimes I wonder how the world goes on without Justin in it and I question everything. Why does the sun still come up? How can people drive to work and continue with life? Don't they know my son died? The whole world should have been unable to function without his beautiful face, amazing blue eyes, his contagious laugh and the greatest hugs on the planet.

Justin is gone, but so much of him lives on—and not just in a figurative sense. Eleven months before the accident, my father died while waiting for a donor heart. Justin made it clear that if anything happened to him, we were to donate his organs. We did just that, donating his heart, lungs, liver, pancreas, kidneys, corneas and tissues. Through his death, he saved the lives of five people and gave sight to two. In fact, his liver was split and donated to different people—an older woman and a six-year-old boy! I've been able to meet the woman who received his heart. She is a wonderful, lovely lady who I feel is very worthy of the "Gift of Life." There are no words to describe the comfort that comes from knowing that my son's heart is still beating and that this woman's family, including her three sons, have been spared the grief of losing a loved one. She told the newspapers that when she found out her heart came from a fifteen-year-old boy, she would have gladly traded places with him. When we met, I kept touching her chest over her heart to feel its beat. That heart has now been in three bodies—mine, Justin's and hers. I presented her with a photo album of Justin so she would know whose heart beats inside her.

A lot of Justin's friends still come by, including his girl-friend. They get together and swim in our pool. We always laugh when they arrive and say, "Justin is having another pool party." I believe it's a tribute to him that they still visit us. I guess coming over and talking about Justin with his family helps his friends to heal as well. Sometimes though, I worry about Justin's girlfriend. Justin was a one-in-a-million boyfriend, very charming and attentive. They were so very much in love and she has taken his death very hard. I pray for her everyday, hoping that she'll move forward with her life and become a happy, strong adult.

Justin's accident left our family with a big piece of the puzzle missing. His father and I can't get through an hour without talking about him. We miss him with every fiber of our beings. His baseball bag remains packed in his room, waiting for the next practice.

A parent's worst fear is that his or her child will be for-gotten. That night in the intensive care unit, as I prayed from the depths of my soul for God to spare my child, I knew that

Justin's purpose on earth was over—and that my purpose was just beginning. I had to find a way to honor my precious child. Contributing Justin's story to this book, along with my volunteer work for L.O.P.A. (Louisiana Organ Procurement Agency) have done wonders for my grief recovery. For these things, I will be eternally grateful.

Justin's Contacts

Justin hasn't blatantly appeared or spoken to me yet, but I often have this overwhelming feeling that he's around. I felt this way one day when I was walking along our property. I was about to cross over a spot where I walk every day without so much as a thought when I suddenly stopped. I felt Justin's presence, then a strange thought popped into my mind. *Boy, this looks snakey!* Unsure where it came from, I tossed the thought aside and continued walking once more. Again, for some reason, I stopped dead in my tracks. I eased forward, then saw it—a poisonous snake was slithering toward the exact spot where I would have been had I not stopped twice. I give Justin credit for possibly saving my life.

At his grave one day, I began pulling the grass from around the edges of his marker while at the same time talking to him. The wind was blowing hard and steady and a large, brightly colored pinwheel I'd placed in the ground was spinning rapidly. "Oh Justin, I miss you so much," I said. The pinwheel suddenly stopped. The cemetery's flags were still flapping and the chimes were singing, but the pinwheel was frozen. After a moment, it started up again. Then, when I resumed speaking to Justin, it stopped. Every time I told him that I loved him or missed him, the wheel would start whirring wildly, then freeze. The wind was blowing strongly and steadily. Nothing else in the cemetery was stopping and starting like that. It was baffling. I tested it for twenty minutes, too stubborn to believe anything supernatural was occurring, yet it continued to happen. A wonderful peace finally washed over me. "Justin, are you trying to tell me you're okay?" I asked. The pinwheel began spinning faster than ever before, then creaked as it stopped. I knew then that no matter how hard I tried to deny it, Justin was indeed communicating with me. I left his grave that day knowing that he was alright.

Both Justin's father and I hear him in the house sometimes. The thump of his feet on the floor is unmistakable as he moves around in his room upstairs. Recently, when we were watching television in the game room, something began tapping on the light fixture. These kinds of things have become so normal to me that I didn't even blink. I simply said, "I love you, too, Justin."

– Libbie Harrison

The loss of a loved one is probably the most stressful event a person can experience. However, the anguish is that much greater when the loss is both sudden and of a child. It may take years and years to begin healing. The healing eventually came for Beverly Reed, but it was slow and only with the help of the very child she lost.

Jessica was born on her father's thirty-third birthday—June 1, 1994. It was the best birthday present I could give my husband, Ken. She was our third daughter. Our finances had improved enough for us that I could quit my job and become a full-time mother to our growing family.

From the very beginning, Jessica had spunk. She was always getting herself into trouble. She loved to hide and enjoyed creating crayon artwork on our freshly painted walls. No car seat could hold her, so I had to tie her shoelaces together to try and get her to stay put. It took her one ride to learn that if she took her shoes off, she could escape as before. Mischievous as she was, she was easy to love. Her smiles and laughter lit up our house.

On Sunday, January 5, 1997, I told the kids after dinner they could play for a while before I put them to bed. Jessica sat with her father for a few minutes, then wandered upstairs around 8:30 P.M. and went into the room she shared with her sister, Samantha. My oldest daughter, Trisha, also went upstairs with Samantha right behind her. Samantha and Trisha played video games in Trisha's room. Being mischievous as usual, Jessica grabbed her favorite books and took the opportunity to climb up to the top bunk where Samantha slept. This was a special thrill because we had just given the girls the brand new bunk beds for Christmas. My husband had built it for them himself.

Jessica plopped on her stomach, put her feet between the safety bars and mattress and began flipping through a book. She must have gotten bored, because she decided to get down off the top bunk. Instead of using the ladder, she tried to squeeze her body between the tiny space that separated the bars. She quickly became trapped. The weight of her body pulled her lower and the bars eventually cut off the air to her throat.

I went upstairs at 8:45 to tuck the kids in and bring Jessica her "blanky." I walked into her room and said, "Jessi, look what I...." I never finished the sentence. A normal, cheery, family moment had transformed into a living nightmare. The lifeless form of my baby hanging from the bunk bed was the most horrifying image I have ever seen or could ever imagine. It's something I'll never forget.

I tried CPR and when they arrived, the police and paramedics did all they could, but real life isn't like television. They can't save everybody.

Ken, Trisha, Samantha and I lost the centerpiece of our family. Jessica was like a bubbly soda that made our daily lives sparkle. At first, after she died, we walked around like zombies. No one talked. We just cried. We tried going to a therapist, but the sessions we attended were not very helpful. The counselor had never personally experienced a close family death and was overwhelmed by the volcanic grief the four of us were experiencing. I began searching the Internet for help and one day I found a Web site called "Web-healing." This site became my lifeline. It was a virtual world where everybody was dealing with grief caused by one kind of loss or another. They reached out to us and each other with the message, "What you are feeling is normal." The group guided me in my mourning by offering unconditional support and understanding.

Through "Web-healing," I met a wonderful woman who is my age and was suffering through the same emotional trauma as I was. Her seven-year-old daughter had been killed in a traffic accident. This woman and I became best friends.

It's sad to say, but my husband Ken has not faired too well. He has been tormented by the guilt of having built the bunk beds. Ken feels responsible for the accident that killed his daughter. No one has been able to convince him otherwise. The police officers who checked the bed that night said it was no different than any other bunk beds they've examined, that all bunk beds have the same design flaw regarding the railings. I try to be as supportive as I can and I'm there for him when my husband needs me. The therapist said it will take time before Ken will be able to forgive himself. I just wish I could take his pain and guilt away.

Our daughters are recovering as well as can be expected. The therapist told us that children rebound faster than adults and this seems to be true in our case. However, Samantha is autistic and her level of understanding is different than ours, so it's difficult to assess whether or not she truly understands what happened and how well she is coping with the loss. For example, moments before I entered the room and found Jessica's body, Samantha told me that Jessi was asleep in her bed. I believe Samantha may have seen what I saw, but had difficulty processing what happened to her sister.

For me, Jessica's death has been very hard. One coping mechanism I've developed involves an enhancement of my senses. It's hard to explain. It's as if my five senses are heightened. For example, when a person is talking out of earshot, if I concentrate hard enough, I will be able to hear them. Also, I see flashing images of what appear to be photos and when I describe them to people who I think will understand their meaning, they are shocked and amazed by my visions. I don't know why I'm experiencing this. I just know that this phenomena has comforted me when I've felt that I've hit bottom.

Jessica's Contacts

The morning after Jessica passed, Samantha woke up in a panic. She called out, "Mommy! Mommy!" I ran downstairs where she was sleeping in a spare room. "Mommy! Mommy! I show you Jessica!" she said when I came in. I broke down in tears as she grabbed my hand and took me back upstairs to the room she had shared with Jessica. "Mommy, please get Jessi down!"

"I can't, Sam. Jessi is gone."

Sam led me to the window and pointed out to the sky. "Mom, that okay. Jessi went through here into the sun." With that, she calmly walked out of the room and went downstairs, obviously at peace. I collapsed to the floor, sobbing uncontrollably. Jessi died at night, so the light Sam saw couldn't have been the sun. Furthermore, the moon was not visible through the window in Sam and Jessi's room. There was no natural light in the sky for Samantha to have seen that night. I'm convinced that Jessica took a few minutes to show Sam that she was going home to heaven and allowed Sam to watch her walk into God's light.

Although Sam and Jessi were very close, Sam has never once asked where her sister is. If I ask her about it, she says in a matter-of-fact voice, "Jessi in heaven." I attribute her certainty to the wonderful vision she experienced.

On the night of Jessica's burial, I asked the Heavenly Father to help me find the strength to go on with my life so I could take care of my other children. Although my eyes were shut, everything seemed to get much blacker. Then, a tiny pinpoint of light appeared in the distance. It began to rapidly expand. It was as if I was looking through a telescope that was out of focus. Suddenly, Jessica came into clear view. She was wearing a beautiful white dress and had flowers in her hair. She was running towards a light. Before reaching it, she turned around and I heard her voice in my head say, *Thanks for the pop, Mommy!* In her hand was her favorite lollipop. I was confused for a moment, then realized that I had placed the lollipop in her coffin with her! Jessi turned back around and vanished into the light. The moment was extremely brief, but so powerful and comforting. I cried so incredibly hard after the vision—not out of grief, but out of the joy; joy of knowing that my daughter was not in the ground, but in the loving world of heaven waiting for me to be with her again one day. For me, a mother, nothing is more comforting than knowing my child is safe and happy.

Recently, I had one of the most vivid contacts from Jessica yet. I put Samantha to bed and went into my room to watch a movie. Shortly thereafter, I heard Sam's toy piano playing. I didn't give it much thought, because I assumed Sam had woken up and was playing with it. However, it kept going on and on. Then I heard singing. That caught my attention, because it sounded just like Jessi. I got out of bed and headed down the hall to see what was going on. The singing and piano playing continued right up until I entered the room, then they abruptly stopped. When I turned the corner, I was shocked to find Sam fast asleep! The piano was in its regular spot at the foot of the bed with no sign of having been moved or touched. It had to have been Jessi! It was a comforting sign that Jessica was still around watching over her older sister. She and Sam were best friends—and, apparently, they still are.

– Beverly Reed

Upon hearing the unwelcome news that a child has died, the world seems to stop for a parent who often wonders how to find the strength to go on. A parent may even feel guilty for moving on with life. However, one of the greatest ways we can honor our lost loved ones is to cherish their memories while still leading full lives. As Gail Sangregorio relates, she has been able to do just that with the help of dreams and other events that have proven to her that her son lives on in another world.

Two police officers came to our home just before midnight on November 30, 1990. Our daughters, Cheri and Karen, were watching television when they heard the fateful knock at the door. They ran into our room to awaken my husband, Bob, and me. Cheri later said she saw tears in my eyes even before we reached the door where the officer waited. All I remember hearing was, "Greg Robert Sangregorio." Before the officers could finish, mentally, I was gone—gone to a place I don't remember.

My dear Greg was an athletic twenty-year-old with everything to live for. He was the oldest of our three children and my only son. Greg was extremely close to his twin sisters, who were born just a little more than a year after he was. At six-feet, four-inches, he had been the basketball star in high school. His interests turned to acting and drama in college. He spent his last evening ushering for an event staged by his theater class. On Greg's way home, an intoxicated man lost control of his car which jumped across the traffic lanes and hit Greg's vehicle head-on, taking him from us forever. The man died as well, burning up in his own vehicle.

My family told me later that I screamed for a very long time when the police told me the news. When I finally stopped, I was lost. Yet, ironically, I soon felt that everything would one day be all right. Not to say that my son's death wasn't horrible, but through all the anguish, synchronistic and serendipitous events began to sustain and comfort me and allow me glimpses into the usually unseen world.

I've coped by, among other things, writing poems, including "She-Bear," which has been used in various grief therapy programs. It chronicles the start of my nine-year odyssey of bereavement. "She-Bear" speaks of the severe isolation in burying someone we love.

What have I learned in these long years without Greg? I've learned that refusing to live my life dishonors him; that a lost loved one cannot remain the center of one's life; that even though you don't know what God is doing, He does; that a death is not a punishment; that our senses betray us; that our beloved lives on in our hearts and in heaven.

When I learned that Greg had been killed, I felt like my head cracked open, yet it was only then that I became sane. I was forced to push away an old belief system that was maladaptive. The past died along with my previous persona. I was no longer a scared little rabbit. I grew up—all in that instant.

Greg's Contacts

The night after Greg died, I had an intense dream. I was on Lake Michigan Drive, at the precise spot where my son perished. I saw the accident, the flashing red lights, the other driver and a host of filmy looking people who appeared to be spirits. Oddly enough, all but one of these spirits were assisting the drunken driver who caused the accident, ushering his soul away from his exploding vehicle. Greg's soul was standing outside his car accompanied by a single spirit that appeared to be my uncle Jim. I was hysterical and screamed at Greg to get back inside his body, which was slumped behind the wheel. With great tenderness, he said, "I can't do that, Mom. You must remember that we all agreed to this before we came here."

I instantly understood what he meant. We—my family—were together in some spiritual form prior to our existence on earth. During the planning of our sojourn here, it was decided that Greg would only be with us for twenty years. When he came to me in the dream, he reminded me that this was his predestination and that I should accept it. I believe this is the unremembered place I went to when I was first told of his death.

The way the dream ended has troubled me for more than a decade. We were flying, hand in hand, to the dark side of the moon. I don't know how and when we parted, but when I was alone I became fearful that I'd gone too far in this surreal journey and might have injured myself in the process. Then I woke up.

On the one year anniversary of his death, Cheri, Karen and I placed a cross his father made on the side of the road where Greg died. We took some pictures and headed back to the car. As we began driving away, Karen noticed that there was a single shot left in the camera, so she snapped it from the moving vehicle. When this photo was developed, the tree branches formed a startling figure that looked just like Greg wearing his hat. In addition, there appeared to be an angel looking out toward the road. We all viewed this photo as more evidence of Greg's ongoing existence.

– Gail Sangregorio

Another family who has found comfort and healing through contact with their lost son are the Mundts. Their story emphasizes the need for friends and relatives to express concern and love for the parents left behind. When family members and friends don't acknowledge the child's life and death as well as important dates—birth date, death date— their actions often inadvertently add to the parents' grief.

One of our family traditions is to camp out each September at the local fair grounds during the annual State Fair. Our grandparents almost always pull up in their camper and join us. For years, we've spent Labor Day evening watching the big talent show that highlights the annual extravaganza.

The year 1994 marked the first time my son Matt asked to bow out of the celebration. He was a teenager and wanted to spend the last days of summer with his friends. My husband and I were reluctant, especially since Matt had just bought a car and had only been driving for a year. He was a good kid, an honor student, athlete and law buff who dreamed of becoming an attorney one day. He was responsible and levelheaded, so we concluded that we really had no reason to deny his wishes.

Matt's younger brother, Chris, often went places with his older brother and Matt's friends, but this time, Matt refused to bring his little brother along, instead dropping Chris off at the fair. Chris was pretty angry about it, but Matt clearly made his choice: there would be no fourteen-year-old brother hanging around that night.

The evening proceeded as normal. We walked around the fairgrounds enjoying the sights, then headed back to the camper. From a distance, I could see that someone had left a note on the windshield. This wasn't unusual at the fair, as friends and relatives routinely left messages in that manner. When we arrived at the camper, my husband read the note and frowned. "It says we're supposed to phone the hospital," he told me. Chris and I followed him as he went to a pay-phone to call the number left on the note. We were shocked to learn that Matt had been in an auto accident. His condition was described as "grave."

After screaming in unison, we jumped in the car and sped to the hospital, uttering the Lord's Prayer the whole way. The news was even worse when we arrived. Matt had rolled his car, was thrown from the vehicle and suffered critical head injuries. In contrast, his two best friends who were with him in the car escaped untouched. It appears that they were wearing their seat belts and Matt wasn't.

Inside the intensive care unit, I held Matt's hand as the doctors struggled to save his life. I remember how cold his body felt. The doctors said it was because he'd lost so much blood. The chill of his skin unnerved me so much I just cried and cried. I sensed his pain and soon found myself saying to him, "Go live with Jesus." The instant I said that, his cold hand grew warm and his body quaked as if his soul was leaving. He opened his eyes, acknowledged his brother Chris's whispered goodbye, then passed on to the next world.

Our immediate family has subsequently been in counseling. We were fortunate to find an excellent grief therapist who helped us deal with our shattered lives. We've discussed many issues, especially those concerning drinking. Although Matt had not been drinking that evening, his friends had. Apparently, the interaction going on inside the car was enough to distract Matt and cause him to lose control. People should understand that even with a "designated driver" things can go terribly wrong when passengers in a car are intoxicated. I feel strongly about not only the issue of drinking and driving, but drinking and being a passenger. Kids tend to live life with no fear of the consequences. They think they are indestructible and will never die. On the other hand, the peer pressure on kids to drink is very strong. I just hope that they see the pain their actions can lead to before other tragedies occur.

It has not been easy as a parent to go through these things, especially since I have younger children facing the same pressures Matt faced as they enter their teens. I just try to do my best to teach them right from wrong and hope they make good choices when it comes to peer pressure and drinking.

Aside from the therapist and each other, my immediate family has not had a lot of support getting through this tragedy. I love my extended families on both sides, but many of my relatives seem so uncomfortable with the issue of Matt's death and our grief that they've practically ignored my son's death. I don't know what's worse, Matt's death and our missing him or the fact that some family members don't even acknowledge his life anymore. This has been one of the hardest parts of the grief for us. Few, if any, relatives talk about Matt. They don't even want to be around us much. It appears to be such an effort for them to be with us. I realize everyone grieves in his or her own way, but family members should be there for their relatives—even if those relatives are adults—when they're in so much pain. I want and need to talk about Matt, but they don't want to listen. I feel so emotionally abandoned. Since Matt's death, I've wondered if others in this kind of situation have experienced the same problems with their families and I truly hope they haven't.

Matt's Contacts

One of the highlights of the State Fair is a raffle drawing for the Grand Prize. My kids and my parents try to win it every year with no luck. The odds are stacked against them, because it's a huge fair with thousands of eager participants.

The night we lost Matt, however, my daughter Chelsey's number was called out and she won. Her matching ticket was pulled at 5:38 P.M. and she was presented with a "really neat" sitting bench with an American flag on it. When I later read the police report, I was shocked to see it stated that Matt's accident happened at 5:38 P.M. We all feel that this was Matt's final gift to his sister and was his way of telling Chelsey he would always be with her.

Two nights later, Matt appeared to his brother Chris in a vivid dream. Matt told Chris that he was in heaven and was okay. Chris reported that Matt laughed and said, "God is so cool. He wears a baseball cap!"

The most amazing contact from Matt was reported by my great-grandmother. She's a very devout Christian woman who doesn't go for anything that veers from the biblical straight and narrow. A month after Matt's funeral, I called to check in with her and lean on her strong shoulder. Through it all, she had served as our strength and wise counsel. She told me to have my husband pick up the other telephone extension and then very reluctantly, she informed us that she had seen Matt. She hesitated in telling us, she said, because she thought we might think she was crazy or that we would get upset. We assured her that neither was the case. She went on to explain that she had just crawled into bed and began reading her daily devotions when Matt appeared in the room surrounded by light. She described the clothes he was wearing and I recognized them as the ones he had selected for his school pictures—photographs she had not yet seen. "He was smiling and happy," she reported, "and wanted me to 'tell mom and dad that I'm okay.' Then he faded with the light."

I believe that God allows us these special times so that our loved ones can tell us in their own ways that they are in heaven and are alright.

– Patti Mundt

Though some individuals might think adoptive parents and their children aren't as closely bonded as biological ones, the following story proves otherwise. Love transcends biological or cultural ties. Even death has not broken the bond between Bob Coe and the adopted son he lost.

I adopted Mike when he was seven years old. It wasn't the ordinary family situation. I'm a single man. I had previously adopted an older teenager who had been my "little brother" in the Big Brother program. This child was seventeen when I started the process of adopting another child and he was almost nineteen when Mike was added to our family. They say it's tough to adopt older children because their behavior patterns are already set. I guess I never listened to that.

Mike was a darling, charming, sweet boy who had suffered through considerable emotional trauma. He and his younger brother and sister had been removed from their mother by Child Protective Services for reasons they didn't disclose. They were placed into foster care. The foster parents ended up adopting his infant siblings, but not Mike. They didn't feel they could handle Mike's needs—he was beyond the prime age for adoption.

Mike was dealing with pretty heavy feelings of rejection for quite a while after he came to live with us. My older son and I countered that by showering him with love and attention. It wasn't long before those paralyzing feelings of being unwanted were washed away. Mike transformed into a happy, well-adjusted child who easily made friends. He played soccer, baseball and did all the typical kid things.

When he entered adolescence, he started having some emotional problems. This is typical of older adopted children and is one of the reasons prospective parents shy away from them. In Mike's case, he started having flashbacks of things that had happened when he was little. He frequently came into my room at night in tears, frightened by a dream or a sudden dark memory. He rarely mentioned what specifically had frightened him, preferring to keep the horror locked inside. One night, after a particularly vivid flashback, he broke down and told me that his mother's boyfriend used to throw burning matches at his legs to make him "dance." He lifted his pajama pant leg and showed me the scars this abusive game had caused, then sobbed uncontrollably for a long time.

When Mike was twelve, I adopted another little boy, Arthur, who was six. This addition to my growing family went pretty smoothly. As I saw it, the more the merrier. Three years later, a social worker begged me to take in a sixteen-year-old foster son whose mother was terminally ill. This youth, Shirden, was with us only two weeks when his mother died, so it was a very emotional time for him. Still, with all these seeming negatives, the boys all got along very well and became fast friends. They acted just like birth siblings, playing one minute, arguing and fighting the next, but always wanting to be together. And since Mike and Shirden were close to the same age, they became the best of friends.

Late one afternoon of the following year, Mike and Shirden hopped on their bikes and didn't come back for hours. I went out looking for them, but they were nowhere to be found. It wasn't unusual for the pair to take off on one of their adventures, so I suppressed my concern and went to bed, figuring they were spending the night at a friend's house. As it turns out, they were at a party. The boys eventually had enough and decided to pedal home around 1:00 A.M. There's a train track a block from my house. The boys reached the tracks at the same time a train was about to thunder through. In typical, indestructible, teenage fashion, Mike decided he was going to race the train. "I'm going to beat it!" he cried. As Shirden screamed "Noooooo!" Mike put his head down and shot forward, playing a deadly game of chicken with the massive iron horse. Right before he hit the tracks, he realized he wasn't going to make it and skidded the bike to a stop. He slid further than anticipated, enabling the engine to clip his front wheel, knocking him fifty feet through the air. Although he was unhurt during the "flight," he landed hard on his head and back, suffering severe injuries.

Mike had borrowed the bike from his aunt and left the house wearing her helmet. However, when he exited the party, for some reason he decided not to wear the protective head gear during the trip home.

The police called me within minutes of the accident. I was so close that I arrived at the scene before the ambulance. Mike was on the ground being treated by a paramedic. I wanted so badly to hold him, but they wouldn't let me get close at so critical a time. I motioned for Shirden to get into the car and together we followed the ambulance to the hospital. I was still in my pajamas and had to call my father to bring me some clothes.

It was a horrible night. Mike was injured too severely to be treated, much less saved. He never left the emergency room and died around 4:00 A.M. After that, while I was still in shock, I had to endure the agony of informing Arthur, along with family and friends, of Mike's death. That was tough.

The memorial service was held at the high school. Nearly 800 people attended, with ages ranging from five to ninety years old. It was a tremendous show of affection and support.

Shirden held up as best he could, then completely gave out a few weeks later. He fell into a deep depression that triggered "post traumatic psychosis." He began hearing voices—usually his mother's—and became suicidal. The combination of his mother's death and watching his best friend get hit by a train knocked him over the edge. He had to be hospitalized for several days, which was another scary time for the family. Fortunately, with the proper treatment and medications, he completely recovered.

I put all the boys, including myself, into therapy to help us deal with our grief. That was beneficial, but in the long run, the best therapy was our support for each other. That and the comfort we received from our friends and neighbors helped us recover. They were unbelievable. We didn't cook a meal for six months, because every day someone came over and stuffed the refrigerator with food. Others organized a house cleaning party and went room by room scrubbing, polishing and vacuuming. Four families in particular stayed in touch every day. I don't think I could have made it without them.

Some positives came out of this that have helped cut through the grief. The depth of commitment displayed by our friends was touching. We found friends we didn't even know we had. Internally, our family bonded closer together than ever, each of us making concerted efforts to do the little things that made our collective lives better. We joined forces to put in a new patio, plant flowers around the outside of the house and go on many family trips.

To survive and heal, you do what you can.

Mike's Contacts

I had a vivid dream about three weeks after Mike died. It was so real that it has impacted me greatly. In the dream, I was floating and, at the same time, sitting at a table. Mike was across the table. He didn't speak. I kept trying to reach out and touch him, but I couldn't. Even though he remained silent, he was able to convey to me that he was okay and that he loved me. I kept reaching out for him, but was unable to make physical contact. When he finally disappeared, I felt so much better than before.

I've never really decided in my own mind whether this was truly a contact or just a dream. I do know its effect upon me has remained overpowering.

At Mike's memorial service, my brother, sister-in-law and a few of their friends were kind enough to use their musical talents to play Pachelbel's "Canon in D," a beautiful piece of classical music. Several months after Mike's death, we were all eating out in a nice restaurant with friends when that same song came over the restaurant's muted speakers. After just a few bars, I sensed Mike's presence among us. I looked at Arthur and could tell by his visible reaction that he felt it as well. It was so powerful and real, beyond anything we'd experienced before or since. It didn't last long, only a few short minutes, but we've never forgotten it.

– Bob Coe

Adopted or birth child, car accident or bike accident, parents' grief is profound and deep especially when the death is sudden, unexpected and senseless. Time and supportive family and friends help these parents heal. Yet, sometimes only something as powerful as an after death contact can give them the strength to get through their pain and find healing. Messages from a lost child can transform a horrifically painful loss into a healing, transcendent experience. In experiencing such powerful, mystical encounters, these parents are not alone as the stories in the next chapter reveal.

Chapter Three

Heartbreaking Passings, Uplifting Messages

Whether a child is lost suddenly to an accident or over time to a serious illness, bereaved parents are left crying, "Parents aren't supposed to outlive their children!" However, their pain is alleviated when they hear from their departed children and know that in the next life, those children are safe and content. Linda Zeliger is one parent who agonized over the tragedy of her son's death and found healing through after death contact with her son.

My son and only child, Keith, was a perfectly normal boy, very active, happy, completely healthy—or so I thought. He had blonde hair, sparkling blue eyes and one of the biggest, most beautiful smiles I had ever seen. He started and ended each day as upbeat as could be. He loved to play with anything that had wheels—toy cars, trucks, bikes and motorcycles. He slept in my husband's and my bed from the day he was born. We were inseparable.

On May 22, 1998, I put my adorable three-year-old down for a nap. About an hour later, I went to check on him. At that moment, Keith woke up and looked at me. "Mommy, my head tickles," he said before closing his eyes, never to open them again. I called 911 when I realized he was unconscious. Keith was rushed to the hospital, but nothing could be done to save him. The doctors told me that Keith had a brain stem hemorrhage known as arteriovenus malformation. It was a congenital ticking time bomb no one knew was there. I was devastated beyond belief.

I completely altered my lifestyle after my son's death. I found myself going "back to the basics" in everything I did. Material possessions have no meaning for me anymore. Nothing else that happens for the rest of my life can hurt me, because I've already been hurt beyond compare. Other people can resolve their problems and find ways to ease their various pains, but not me. I can never have my child back.

After Keith's death, I began to feel a deep yearning to help those in need, especially the sick and dying. Although it sounds noble and selfless, my desire to help others was due in part to my own selfish needs. I wanted to be around the dying because I hoped that maybe, as they crossed over to the other side, they would see my Keith and tell me that he's alright, safe and secure in the arms of the Lord.

Keith's Contacts

The night Keith was buried, I fell into a deep sleep. A few hours later, my eyes suddenly popped open and I sat up in bed. I saw Keith hovering near the ceiling in the corner of the room. It was pitch black and my baby appeared inside a circle of light that illuminated him from the shoulders up. The eerie light did not brighten the rest of the room. Keith looked at me and smiled. Behind him were a pair of small wings. They were so clear I could see each individual feather. I tried to reach out to him, but he vanished.

A few weeks later, I was sitting outside on the deck with my mother. We heard a strange noise that sounded like a puppy barking. Mom thought it was coming from somewhere in the neighborhood, but my ears told me it was emanating from inside the house. We walked slowly through the door, nervous about what we might find. It was quiet for a moment, then another wave of sounds startled us. We tracked it down to Keith's electronic story book. It was going off on its own. When I inspected it, I was startled to realized the book was filled with the recorded sounds of cars and trucks—not puppies or dogs. Keith always liked dogs and had begged to have a puppy of his own.

When he was alive, Keith had always enjoyed pushing my key chain to make the car alarm go off. Even in death, Keith enjoys doings this. On September 1, 1998, I was sitting in the car and the alarm sounded. Later that afternoon, as I was trying to get into the car, the locks kept snapping down each time I tried to unlock the door. This had been another of Keith's favorite tricks. "Silly boy," I said as I'd always done. "Please let Mommy into the car." With that, the locks popped back up.

Though his death has been devastating, I am thankful for the contact I have since had with him. I believe that one reason Keith came back to me so quickly was that he was still a toddler when he died and we were so closely connected. I feel he also sensed that my pain was intense and knew I needed his help to find peace.

Keith's contacts have helped; they have brought me comfort and have enabled me to go on. This whole experience has brought me closer to God. However, I am not ready to let go of my son quite yet. Searching for him everywhere, I still pray every night to see Keith once more.

– Linda Zeliger

For most parents, the thought of watching their child fight a devastating, drawn-out illness before succumbing to it is too

*awful to imagine. The next story tells how such an experi-
ence, followed by the lost child's contact from beyond the
wall of death, brought a family closer together.*

My son Tobin was born on March 8, 1995. With his light
hair, big blue eyes, wit, charm and spunk, he was truly a
wonderful child. When he got a little older and his personality
truly developed, he became so serious at times that my husband and I affectionately called him "our little old man." But
even when he was serious, he exhibited an unusually dry sense
of humor. He loved to play jokes on his daddy and prepare
food with me. Like Linus in the "Peanuts" comic strip, he had
a favorite blanket he dragged around which he named "Bebe."

When Tobin was two, we decided to move from
California to Texas where my husband had a job waiting. We
packed up and headed out on the road. During the trip,
Tobin became ill. His eyes looked bruised and his skin grew
very pale. I thought he had a bad flu. The following day, he
became even sicker and started screaming from the pain. We
pulled over and took him to a hospital. To our shock, on July
21, 1997, we were told our little boy had a type of cancer
called neuroblastoma.

Tobin went through eight months of chemotherapy,
which I quickly learned is incredibly painful and difficult to
endure, especially for a small child. Despite the pain and
sickness, Tobin handled it like a prizefighter, battling the
whole way and doing his best to remain upbeat and cheerful.
His attitude was infectious; everyone around him did their
best to keep his spirits high. The nurses doted on him; his
dad sneaked pizza to him so he could pick off the circles of
pepperoni and eat them with his little fingers; his grandma,
my mother, read his favorite book to him over and over, and
when his other grandma, Jeanie, arrived, she promised to
take him to the beach when he got better.

Yet despite all his cheer and determination, Tobin's condition was not improving. The doctors felt he needed a bone marrow transplant. Tobin's big brother, five-year-old Nolan, courageously volunteered to be the donor. Just over six months after Tobin first entered the hospital, the doctors extracted marrow from Nolan's hips and placed it in a medical bag. This bag was then hooked to Tobin's port—a tube that went into an artery near his heart. Tobin handled the procedure the best he could, even though the powerful medicines he was given to kill his own cancerous marrow made him very ill.

Two weeks later, Tobin suddenly stopped breathing. The doctors and nurses were able to get him breathing again, but he suffered a similar episode the following day. Tobin was brought into the intensive care unit, put on a respirator and kept heavily sedated so he wouldn't pull out his tubes. On February 16, his condition rapidly deteriorated. We were called to his bedside, where the doctors told us a fungus had taken control of Tobin's body, making his blood too acidic to be "conducive with life." At 7:55 the following morning, Tobin passed away. I am thankful we were able to be there to hold him and say our good-byes.

Prior to Tobin's illness, my husband Dave and I were having marital difficulties. I had been miserable, because I felt trapped at home with three young children. But when Tobin became ill, everything changed. Dave and I really bonded as a couple and the family came together. We began going to church together and gained a new sense of being a team. Dave started a business so he could be home every night and spend more time with me and the kids. He soon gained an understanding of what I had been going through before—of how hard it can be to parent three small children. That enabled him to appreciate me more and stop taking me for granted. I, in turn, learned how much I loved and needed him and stopped being so resentful, mean and crabby. We learned to prioritize and reevaluate what was really important in our lives—which we discovered was our desire to simply be together. I know that in some cases, the emotional strain of a child's death causes couples to split up. Ironically, Tobin's illness and eventual death seemed to have the opposite effect upon us. It brought us back together.

This is not to say we weren't devastated by Tobin's death. Our sadness has been overwhelming. We miss Tobin dearly, but we have gained so much from the experience; we gained each other.

I've also gained in other ways since Tobin's death. I have become active in volunteer work for various projects related to childhood cancer, including the construction of a quilt that helps promote awareness. My volunteering has brought me a sense of accomplishment and satisfaction knowing my work may help other children and their families. It has also been cathartic, giving me a place to channel my grief and turn it into something constructive. Yet nothing has given me as much comfort as getting signs from Tobin that tell me his spirit is still with us and that he's gone to a better place.

Tobin's Contacts

A few days after Tobin arrived in the intensive care unit, a group of five pigeons began spending their days on the windowsill just outside his room. They came and went, but never seemed to be bothered by the activity in the room. Yet at the very moment Tobin died, the five pigeons became startled by something in the room and suddenly flew away. Whatever scared the birds must have made an indelible impression on them, because the nurses have told me the birds have never returned. This was the first of many odd occurrences and contacts we've had with Tobin since his death.

Later that same morning, worn out from the shock and depression of Tobin's death, I collapsed on the couch in our home. All of a sudden, in the corner of my eye, I saw a rustle of wings near the ceiling. Something told me that Tobin was in the arms of his angel and he wanted to make sure we were all okay before he left. After that, I was able to drift off into a comforting sleep.

A week after Tobin died, my mother was asleep in her room. It had been a stressful day, because she had just been forced to put her cat Sam to sleep. Sam had cancer and later caught a deadly fungal infection in her lungs. Sadly, the cat's illness was very similar to what happened to Tobin. At 5:30 A.M., she was awakened by the sounds of a music box playing in her room. It was the music box she had bought for Tobin to soothe him to sleep when he was a baby. She hadn't wound it or even touched it for more than a year, yet it started up and played on its own. She laid there listening to it for a full minute, when the sound finally woke her husband. "What's that?" he asked groggily. Without thinking, my mom answered, "That's Tobin coming to take Sam."

One night about a month later, I found myself struggling to fall sleep. My husband was out of town and I was feeling especially lonely for both him and Tobin. All of a sudden, a strange window-shaped patch of light appeared on the bedroom wall. It was odd, because that wall didn't face any of the room's actual windows. Inside the light were four silhouettes. I recognized them as my grandmother, my uncle and my father-in-law, all of whom had passed away. The fourth, a smaller silhouette, was Tobin. Slowly, Tobin's silhouette became a pulsating, fiery ball of light. Seeming to come off the wall, it left the others behind and approached me. Beside it was a spot of mist that bounced around in an odd, frenetic manner. I was surprised to realize that the form and movement of the mist was identical to that of my Chihuahua, a family pet that had died the week Tobin was diagnosed with cancer. The fireball and accompanying mist stopped right in front of me. The light was still pulsating, but resting aloft in midair. "I love you, Tobin," I said as a comforting peace washed over me. The circular light and madly hopping mist remained before me for about five minutes, then retreated back to the wall into the window of light. The window then faded and disappeared.

Tobin appeared to me a few more times as the lighted ball always accompanied by the misty dog, but never again in as spectacular a fashion as he did the first time.

One evening not long afterward, I decided to sleep on the couch just to get away from the same four bedroom walls. I drifted off and dreamed about Tobin sleeping next to me. His head was covered by his light blue blanket "bebe" the way he always slept. I could actually feel him in my arms, small and solid, curled up under my chin and tight against my chest. I remembered how vividly I smelled him. I inhaled deeply to breathe in his scent. In fact, I sniffed so hard I woke myself up. Even awake, I could still sense and smell him. I felt so at peace, knowing he had been there with me.

– Kay MacDonald

Kay's mother-in-law, Jeanie, is very spiritual and, like Kay, has had several of her own contacts with her grandson, Tobin.

I am a firm believer in a circle of life that is never ending. When I received a late night phone call that Tobin was nearing the end, I called my psychic friend and asked her if she could contact Tobin and talk to him. Although he was still technically alive, Tobin had been hooked up to so many machines and had been in and out of consciousness for so long that I wasn't sure if his spirit was still with us. My friend told me she'd try and we hung up. About ten minutes later, she called back and told me that Tobin was "floating in space," laughing and happy. I was saddened to hear that he had already left us. He also told her there was no pain. Both of his grandpas were waiting for him on the other side.

Knowing he would soon be gone physically as well, I immediately made a plane reservation so I could visit Tobin in the hospital. I longed for the comfort of seeing his little face one more time. When I arrived, I could immediately feel him floating freely and happily around the room just as my friend had described.

Whenever I take Tobin's brother Nolan to the beach—which was one of Tobin's favorite places—Tobin always seems to be there with us. Some people may not believe in after death contacts, but I'm here to say they are real. I miss my grandson and know that in spirit he has come to comfort me.

– Jeanie MacDonald

In an ideal world, the biggest concern of new parents would be which one of them their baby resembles, what brand of diapers to buy or hoping the baby will soon sleep through the night. Looking at their healthy, chubby bundle of joy, they would have no concept of what life would be like if their child was born with a serious illness. But in the real world, things don't always work out the way we hope or expect. The Fallers were given a numbing dose of such a reality with the birth of their son, Christopher.

Two days after our son Christopher was born, we faced our first crisis. He was diagnosed with severe damage to his heart caused by a viral infection. The affliction, called "restrictive cardiomyopathy," made his heart muscles progressively stiffen and become less able to pump blood. The doctor said that he might not make it. Well, apparently

Christopher had other ideas. Despite the illness, the hospitalizations and all the IVs and medications, he crawled and walked right on schedule. He valiantly fought his way to the age of five and started kindergarten with all the enthusiasm of a normal, healthy little boy. He was much loved and admired for his strength and perseverance by his teachers and classmates.

Around Christmas, 1996, he developed severe bronchitis and couldn't return to school until the following March. After that, his heart condition suddenly worsened. The doctors told us the only option was a transplant, but not just any ordinary transplant. Christopher became one of only twenty children in the world to have a very rare surgery known as a heterotopic transplant. The surgeons at Children's Hospital in Pittsburgh left Christopher's own malfunctioning heart in place and, using a donor heart, stitched the two together. The unique procedure was completed on October 8, 1997 and drew national media attention.

Not long after the surgery, Christopher was running up and down the hospital halls, acting like a normal seven-year-old boy. He was eventually released from the hospital and was healing nicely. Just when things seemed to be going well, tragedy struck. Christopher contracted post transplant lymphproliferative disease. This is caused by the dreaded Epstein-Barr virus and can result in tumors. Christopher had to return to the hospital to battle this new enemy. Complicating matters further, his body began rejecting the second heart. On February 3, 1998, both of Christopher's hearts stopped. He was resuscitated by doctors, but was also very ill from tumors that had begun forming in his chest. He was soon placed on chemotherapy to combat the tumors and actually began improving for a while. Then, one night in March, he told my husband, Ron, during a visit to the hospital that he was having trouble breathing. The following day, he was put on a ventilator. On March 10, his twin hearts stopped again. The doctors again brought him back, but we realized he was losing the war. His kidneys failed, he contracted more infections and despite the chemotherapy, new tumors sprouted in his chest. His father was with him when he died on March 24, 1998.

Christopher's Contacts

Our contacts with Christopher did not begin until more than a year after his death. On Thursday, April 30, 1999, at 11:30 P.M., I went downstairs to sleep on the couch, because my husband was snoring. At midnight, I decided to return to the bedroom and the comfort of the bed. I climbed into bed, hugged Christopher's two stuffed animals, including "Busy Baby Beaver," which I have kept on my bed since his death, and snuggled under the covers. Just before I drifted to sleep, I felt a sudden chill. Goose pimples raised over my entire body. Then I heard a little voice whisper in my ear, "Good night." As quickly as they had come, the chill and goose pimples vanished, but an awful, rubber band-like taste remained in my mouth. Initially, I didn't tell anyone about the incident, because I wasn't sure if it really happened or if it was merely wishful thinking.

One evening, a few days later, I laid on the couch to nap. Before going to sleep, I talked to Christopher in my mind, telling him what I'd be doing in the coming week. His birthday was coming up and I wanted him to know that we hadn't forgotten. Suddenly, the same chill that had come over my body a few nights before returned along with the goose pimples. A very fuzzy image of Christopher appeared in my head. "I'll hold you, Christopher," I said out loud, hugging my arms tight to my body. At that moment, I felt his presence in my arms. Then I heard a voice in my mind say, *I'm safe*. I knew without a doubt that this was my little

Christopher talking. As quickly as he had come, I felt the presence move away. I relaxed my arms, letting them lie at my sides and then I heard him say in my mind, *Good night.* When his image began fading from my mind, I called out, "But when can I see you again?"

Soon, he responded in my head. I didn't want him to leave yet so I tried hard to envision him again, hoping I could will him back, but he did not return that night. Afterward, I had that same awful rubber band taste in my mouth again.

A few weeks later, I was lying in bed singing Christopher's bedtime songs in my head. Once again, the chills swept over me. I pushed away "Busy Baby Beaver" and extended my arms for Christopher. Again, I sensed his presence, but not as solidly as before. Still, I felt his hair tickling my chin and neck the way it used to. I heard his voice in my mind say, *Sing me another song, Mommy.* I sang five more of our favorite bedtime songs—"Desperado," "We Three Kings," "Bicycle Built For Two," "Baa Baa Black Sheep" and "Red River Valley."

When I finished singing to him, I sensed his spirit fading. "Can I come see you and be with you?" I asked. As before, he answered, *Soon.* His spirit began to slip away further, but before he disappeared I got a good look at him. I was happy to see that he had a full head of golden hair again. The chemotherapy had caused him to lose his hair before he died. He looked so handsome to me with his shiny locks.

Four days later, I was trying hard to sleep, but my mind was filled with troubling images of Christopher at the hospital. As I lay in the dark, I began speaking to him in my head, apologizing for all the suffering he went through. Feeling depressed by the grim images I conjured, I tried to steer my thoughts toward happier moments, but the darker hospital scenes wouldn't relent. In fact, I next flashed back to one particular evening when Christopher had a severe narcotic withdrawal from all the powerful sedatives being given to him. "I did what I could," I said aloud. "At least I was able to hold you for a while." The next thing I heard was his voice close to my left ear. "Thank you, Mommy." My eyes flew open. Scanning the room, I hoped to get a glimpse of him, but he was gone. That is the last contact I've had with Christopher.

– Maria Faller

Raising a child with special needs can be both challenging and rewarding. At times it may be heartbreaking to see the child struggle and at other times, when a parent watches her child overcome so much, the parent often feels great pride and happiness. The loss of such a special child, as the next story relates, is made all the more unbearable by her achievements. Yet, those brief moments after death in which the once struggling little girl lets her parents know she is safe and happy can restore hope and bring healing.

Being pregnant for the first time was wonderful. I loved every minute of it. Everything went smoothly until the AFP (alphafetoprotein) test, which came back with a possibility of Down's Syndrome. I was crushed and chose to do an amniocentesis to find out for sure. If the need arose, I wanted to be able to prepare for a special child. This test came back normal. A side benefit of the amnio procedure was that the accompanying sonogram revealed that we were having a girl. "Go out and buy frilly things," the nurse said cheerfully on the phone. My husband wanted to name her Jessica and I agreed. I spent the rest of my pregnancy happy as could be, mistakenly assuming that the second test ruled out all possibilities of problems.

The only other pre-birth glitch was that Jess was breech and stayed that way until delivery. I was scheduled for a caesarean section on March 29, 1994, but Jess had her own ideas. I woke up in labor on March 16 at 4:30 A.M. Jess was born five hours later. The first thing I remember saying was, "What a tiny nose you have." Little did I know there was a reason for that. It wasn't until later in the evening that the doctor came and told us that there was something wrong with my baby, some kind of genetic problem. I was crushed. The next day, friends and family came to visit the new mom and baby, unaware that there were any problems. My husband was open about it and explained that she wasn't perfect, but we adored her anyway.

Jess had myriad medical problems right from the start. She was visually impaired, had seizures, was "globally delayed in all areas," suffered from gastrointestinal reflux and often had difficulty breathing. Regardless, she was a joy and we loved her. I cuddled her all day long. She just loved to be held and, despite the problems, was a good baby. When she reached six months, she developed yet another ailment. Whenever she cried, secretions would block her airway and she'd turn blue. Sometimes, she passed out, then started breathing again. Other times, she had trouble breathing for a long time afterward. Every time she started to cry, I immediately went into a panic, worrying that I wouldn't be able to keep her airway cleared. It was like living in a constant state of emergency.

We took her to various hospitals, but none of the doctors could come up with a solution. Instead, they gave us a suction machine to help clear the secretions. It ended up being a Catch-22, because even though the machine cleared her airway, it also scared Jess and made her cry longer and harder.

Our days were spent trying to help her gain normal skills while at the same time working feverishly to keep her from crying. Driving with her in the car became a test to see how fast we could get somewhere before something would upset her. If she cried before we reached our destination, we'd have to pull over, hold her and stay there on the side of the road until she was calm enough to be put back into her car seat. Sometimes, I'd sit with her for more than two hours!

Sleeping was another problem. Jess woke up every night and often stayed up all night long crying. Each night was a struggle. Naturally, we were exhausted dealing with one crisis after another.

Regardless, having a special needs child can be rewarding. Jess was very loving. We were thrilled each time she learned a new skill, no matter how small. When you have such a child, nothing is taken for granted, because everything is so difficult. Because she was so brave and we tried so hard, Jess made us better parents and better people in general.

It took a long time for my baby to laugh, but when she did, the wait was worth it! She was also a major cuddler, never pushing away, just sinking into your chest and warming you all over. She brought a kind of joy into our lives that's hard to explain.

I discovered I was pregnant again a week before Jessica's first birthday. It wasn't a planned event, since we had our hands full caring for Jess, but it worked out for the best. Nicholas arrived on time and everything went well. When Nick was born he had a strong-will and became a handful himself. To say we were tired doesn't quite describe it. I'd feel guilty when Nick cried and I couldn't comfort him because Jess was also crying and her needs, of course, took precedence. Having Nick, however, was a blessing. He was a typical child and gave me the "normal" moments that I needed. Taking him on an outing, for instance, was so different. I only needed a bottle, some diapers and off we went.

Despite her health problems, when she turned three, Jess went off to preschool two mornings a week. An early intervention teacher, who was also, thankfully, her godmother, accompanied her at all times. She perked up, made friends and brought home art projects. The other children helped her. It amazed me how the other children were so understanding and accepting of Jessica's difficulties. Although school was good for her, she became sick more often as she was exposed to whatever illness was going around.

After the holidays, on January 2, Nick was in bed and Jess finally fell asleep on the couch. I took special notice that night of how pretty she looked. She had gorgeous porcelain skin, long, extra-thick eyelashes and a cute little nose. I wanted to touch her and pick her up, but didn't want to wake her. Instead, I took the opportunity to get some sleep myself. At 12:30, I heard her cry. My husband, Luis, sprang up to take care of her. The next sound I heard was Luis running up the stairs and breathing heavily. I thought he was having a heart attack! When he reached me, he told me that Jess wasn't breathing. This had happened many times, but from his reaction I knew it was worse than normal. We both ran downstairs. I picked Jess up, then told Luis to call 911. She felt differently than all the other times. Her lips were cold. I shook her gently. "Open your eyes. Open your eyes," I pleaded. I gave her CPR, but deep down, I was sure she was dead. I picked her up, held her tight and rocked her gently as I sat on the floor. When the paramedics arrived, I told them she was gone. I could see how it upset them.

I held her body and sang all the songs I used to sing

to her, including "You Are My Sunshine." I didn't know what else to do. I wanted to hold her forever. I looked at her hands and feet to memorize them. Luis removed her ankle bracelet. Our priest came and I stayed with her while he gave her the last rites. I said goodbye before her body was taken to the funeral home. Jess was a few months short of her third birthday.

Later, at the funeral home, it tore me up seeing her again. I asked everyone to leave me alone with her. I read her a letter I'd written the night before telling her everything I never got to say and apologizing for all the bad times she went through. I cut a lock of her hair and gave her some of her favorite toys. I kissed her over and over.

After she was buried, I went back to the cemetery late that night. She had been so close to me, but now she seemed so far away. I hated the fact that I couldn't help her anymore. I was used to doing everything for her and now we were separated.

Since Jessica's death, I have filled my days taking care of Nick. He helps me to laugh and smile and to not forget. We have pictures of Jess all around the house and have not changed her room. Nick uses it as his playroom.

Despite my close bond with Nick, my life will never be the same without Jess. I think of her every day. At first, I thought that as time passed, I'd think of her less and less and that eventually a whole day would go by and I wouldn't think of her even once. I know now that will never happen. She's part of me. She's in my heart. I feel blessed to have had her in my life.

We still celebrate Jess's birthday every year. I make a cake and invite family and friends over to remember her birth and life. People bring toys, which we place in a special box and donate to the pediatric unit of our local hospital.

Last year, we collected packs of diapers for the special needs children that are part of a foundation I co-founded for multiply-disabled children. For the foundation, we regularly pass out lily stalks, along with flyers that have Jess's picture on them. They also have the saying: "We can't know why the lily has so brief a time to bloom in the warmth of sunlight's kiss upon its face, before it folds its fragrance in and bids the world good night to rest its beauty in a gentler place. But we can know that nothing that is loved is ever lost and no one who has ever touched a heart can really pass away because some beauty lingers on in each memory of which they've been a part."

Jess is no longer with us, but the day she was born is a wonderful memory. By doing something good for others on that day as the years go by, we celebrate her life.

Jessica's Contacts

Three months after Jess died, I had a very strange and powerful dream. I was inside the house gazing out the front door. I thought I saw snow falling, but when I looked closer, I saw not snow but thousands of little feathers floating down from the sky. I ran to the back door to see if the same thing was happening in the backyard. It was. Then a swirl of bright colors came towards me. The swirl was filled with tiny angels the size of butterflies. One of the angels brought me a large, round globe. There was a figure inside the globe. I felt an overwhelming love for that presence in the globe. The entity said, "I love you," then became my Jessica. "I love you, Mommy!" she said again. I reached out and hugged her. "I love you and miss you," I answered. I opened my eyes wider to see her better. As I was opening them in the dream, I was opening them in reality. Jess faded away.

"Don't forget, don't forget, don't forget," I repeated to myself, not wanting to lose the memory of what I'd experienced. The part that was most wonderful was hearing Jess talk. In life, she had never been able to speak. This was the only time I ever heard her talk and the only time she was able to return a hug. It felt so real. I could actually hear and feel her. I've had other dreams about Jess, regular dreams coming from my own mind, but nothing tangible and sensory like this. I know people will see my dream as "grasping at straws," but I believe this was Jess's way of telling me she's okay.

– Kathy Galbis

Accepting their children's deaths was difficult and even seemingly impossible for many of the parents who shared the previous stories. However, one common thread enabled them all to better cope with their pain than perhaps they would have otherwise: the very children they lost came back to them in visions, dreams and through physical means to let their parents know they are in a better place, a place where the pain and suffering of their illnesses and medical problems no longer plague them.

In the next chapter, more parents share amazing stories that begin with tragedies and end with signs of hope.

Chapter Four

Painful Goodbyes, Touching Returns

More children die from illness than from accidents, according to a survey of bereaved parents sponsored by the Compassionate Friends. The majority of deaths by illness occur in sons and daughters over the age of twenty-one, while accidents claim the lives of most teens. Whether the child is a newborn or fifty-years-old when they die, the pain and heartbreak of burying one's son or daughter is deeply felt by parents. Author Dary Matera's grandmother Connie, tells the following story about the death of her daughter, Dolly, and how it was Dolly who, from beyond the wall of death, helped Connie to break out of her intense grief, cope with the loss and embrace life once again.

Even though she had left the nest more than three decades before and was well into middle age, my daughter Dolly remained the center of my life. My sons, Matteo and Beau, both joined the service in their teens and never lived at home again. Matteo became a foreign service officer for the United States government and spent a large part of his life overseas. I was not only distanced from him, but my three grandchildren as well. Beau headed west, choosing to live under the neon lights of Las Vegas, then later in chilly San Francisco. For me in New York, that was almost as far away as Matteo's homes in Greece and the orient.

Dolly stayed right in good old New York City, never more than an hour's drive from my numerous houses and apartments. Even when I moved out near the sea on Long Island, she was close enough for weekly visits. Not only was it great to have her around, I was able to share the day to day trials and tribulations of at least one of my grandchildren as he went through the formative years of his life. By staying in New York, Dolly gave me the privilege of watching her only child, "Little James," grow from a baby into a man.

My wonderful daughter was always a welcoming port in the storm. Through the years, there were many tragedies in my family. My youngest brother was killed in a traffic accident when he was six. Another brother, Johnny, was shot in a taxicab over a business dispute. A third brother, Frank, died in his early sixties of a sudden heart attack. An in-law, angry at his family over some long forgotten squabble, decided to "get even" by hanging himself on Christmas day. One of my own babies died in his crib at age two. That was long before the term and concept of SIDS (Sudden Infant Death Syndrome) was common, so I was left in shock with no answers to my questions, no doctors to explain how and why such a thing could happen.

During it all, Dolly was always there to get me through the dark days and nights. Without her, I'd have never made it.

After her son, "Little James" left home, I grew closer to Dolly than before. I was a young mother, having had all my children in my teens, so we really weren't that far apart in age. I've always been young at heart and Dolly inherited my happy, laughing spirit. In our later years, we were more like giggling best friends than mother and daughter. Most people who met us thought we were sisters. Those were some of the best years we'd ever had.

Without warning, it was over. An aneurysm in my daughter's chest killed her at age fifty as quickly and suddenly as the bullet that had taken my brother.

Even though violence, tragic accidents and relentless death had been so much a part of my life, my grief over losing Dolly was like nothing I'd experienced before. This was my child, my best friend, my sister, my life. She was the strong shoulder who helped me deal with the loss of all the others. Now she was gone and so was my emotional shield.

I fell into a deep, dark depression that lingered for years. My happy-go-lucky spirit vanished. I saw no reason to get up in the morning. Each new day did nothing but bring more grief over losing my Dolly.

As time passed, my sons returned to my life. When Matteo retired from the service and came back to the United States, I moved into his Florida home. A decade later, Beau retired and moved in with us as well. This, of course, brought me into closer contact with my three "lost" grandchildren— and my three great grandchildren! It was a wonderful turn of events for a "lonely old lady."

Regardless, no matter how hard I tried and how much I told myself to count my blessings, I still couldn't get over losing Dolly. I felt there could be no true joy for me in being with my sons, their children or their children's children as long as Dolly wasn't alive. Instead of realizing how fortunate I was to have so many relatives around during my golden years, I often retreated to my room and shrouded myself in misery. No matter how many people came to visit, they just couldn't hold a candle to my Dolly. The way I saw it, everyone had either left for long periods in the past or, like the grandchildren and their kids, would always leave after brief visits. It wasn't like that back in Italy where I was born or even in the early 1900s in New York. But that's the way America has become. Transportation improved, the world grew smaller and families began to move, move, move, spreading out across the planet. I guess I resented it. So instead of fully embracing my family when they visited, I clung to the memory of Dolly, because she was the one person among my immediate family who had never left me.

Dolly's Contacts

Like most people, I've hung numerous pictures of my family on the walls of my apartment attached to Matteo's home. The biggest one was a huge, twenty-five by forty inch framed, full-length portrait of Dolly and my son-in-law, James, at their twenty-fifth anniversary celebration. The photographer captured them reaffirming their vows. The massive photo hovered over the living room and dominated the surroundings, so much so that many people advised me to take it down. They felt such an overpowering picture did nothing but increase my grief. They were so wrong. That giant photo was the only thing keeping me sane.

Virtually the entire extended family came to Florida for the Christmas holidays one year in the mid 1980s. My granddaughter, a Baptist missionary in South Africa, Germany and Russia, was home for a brief time with her husband and two teenage children, so that year was an extra special occasion. The house was full of life, laughter and children of all ages. It was truly a joyous time for everyone—except me. I was stubbornly having none of it. Instead of joining in, I chose to lock myself in my room and grieve over Dolly. When the holidays passed and most everyone left as usual, I found myself sitting alone on the sofa late one night, sipping tea and bemoaning my fate. I stared at the photo of Dolly. She was still so beautiful, happy and trim despite her age.

All of a sudden, Dolly came to life! She crawled right out of the picture and hopped down upon a display table below. She remained the same size and proportion as she was in the photo—about eighteen inches tall—and was still wearing the formal gown.

"Mom, what's the matter with you?" she said in her always frank style. "You spent the holidays moping around while you had everybody who means anything to you right here in this house. Do you know how many women your age would kill for just one moment like that? You've had chance to be with your grandchildren and your great grandchildren whom you've only seen a few times before. Matty and Beau even live with you now. And still, you can't drag yourself out of this room?"

I was stunned. I couldn't believe it. Not only had my beloved daughter returned—even if it was a miniature version—she was scolding me!

"I just, I just miss you, Dolly. I've never gotten over your death."

"It's been ten years! James has moved on and remarried," she said, nodding back toward the portrait from which she'd emerged and in which her husband now stood alone. "Why can't you get over it and move on, too?"

"It's just so hard for me."

"I want you to stop moping and enjoy the rest of your life, okay? I'm fine, Ma. I'm happy. Don't worry about me so much anymore. You don't have many years left. You'll be with me soon enough, so enjoy all those you have around you now."

"Okay," I promised.

With that, Dolly turned around and jumped right back into the picture and took her place beside her husband.

After that stunning development, I tried many times to call her back. I stared at the photo and begged her to come talk to me again, but she never did. Still, I kept my promise. Although it was hard, I heeded her words, tried my best to put her death behind me and stopped being so miserable when people came to visit. Five years later, my missionary granddaughter returned from overseas again and we had another big celebration. This time, I freely joined in the fun. I've done so ever since, thanks to that eye-opening scolding from my daughter.

– Connie Vocale

Even after her death, Dary Matera never doubted the veracity of his grandmother's story, because there was in fact a remarkable change in her personality and attitude following the time when she said Dolly spoke to her. Connie had grieved terribly for Dolly for more than a decade. Then, as if she had a sudden change of heart, Connie suddenly freshened up her face, hair, clothes and spirit and rejoined her family and her life.

Though she did not have as big a transformation as Connie Vocale, Susie LeMaster did learn a lot about herself when she lost her son, Gerald, to cancer. As she relates in the next story, after Gerald's death, Susie aspired to become a more loving, accepting person—the kind of positive and persevering person her son had been.

My son, Gerald, an outgoing, happy young man of twenty-eight, went to work at a construction site on May 21, 1993 and promptly suffered a grand mal seizure. He was rushed to a local hospital where a team of doctors struggled for hours to stop the frequent and sudden onslaught of frightening, uncontrollable body movements. It was so difficult to treat that they were forced to rush him into surgery at 1:00 A.M. the next morning. Five hours later, two doctors emerged from the operating room and gave me the bad news. Gerald had an inoperable brain tumor. He would be lucky to survive another six months.

The doctors didn't know my Gerald. With radiation treatments, chemotherapy and no small amount of determination, six full years passed and Gerald was still alive. He was unable to work because his short term memory was gone, but he still lived on his own and found ways to be productive and independent. He did odd jobs as a painter, landscaper and whatever else he could find. He wrote poems, letters, songs and created beautiful works of art. He even joined a band, playing guitar and soon became the lead singer. I always thought it funny that his memory problems didn't interfere with his ability to belt out hours of song lyrics.

My beloved son was so brave and positive that his friends came from all over to be with him and help with his care. He kept pushing himself to lead a normal life and did so until his body finally gave out. At that point, he came home to me to die.

I knew my son was dying, but that didn't mean I was going to let him go without one hell of a fight! When the angels came for Gerald, I could see their shadows on the wall. I saw them moving closer toward him. I screamed at them to leave my son alone and they backed off. The problem was, they didn't go far. They hovered behind me as I sat at his side. Whenever I looked away or lost my concentration, they crept closer and I had to scream and scare them off again.

Unfortunately, the angels were not always visible to me. In his final days, Gerald began to recognize his angels and assured me that they were benevolent and kind. He said my father, George, my grandpa, Ray, his uncles C.B. and Baird and his aunt Lucille were among them. He addressed them all by name and would smile and nod toward certain points in the room, obviously seeing things I couldn't. As time passed, his face became paralyzed and his vocal cords froze, so he lost the ability to speak. Yet on his last day, he regained his voice. "Look Mommy, it's Gramps! He's so cute," he said, pointing to an empty spot in the corner. "And there's my great grandpa and that pretty lady, I can't remember her name, she moved in with us a week ago."

Gerald's uncles, aunt, grandfather and great grandfather had long passed away, so those visions weren't surprising. However, the "pretty lady" confused me. I asked him some questions and realized he was describing his Aunt Bonnie, my brother's wife. Bonnie, a tall, striking blonde, had died ten years before. "I like her. She's funny," Gerald said.

On March 25, 1999, Gerald whispered "I love my mommy" a number of times, then went to sleep. When I left the room for a few moments, the spirits took advantage of the opportunity. While I wasn't there to protect him, Gerald was taken away by the angels.

I was angry at first, but realized the angels had to do it. Gerald suffered terribly for so long. Although it shames me to admit it, I realized Gerald clung to life those last months just for me. He knew that I just couldn't bear to let him go.

In retrospect, I'm grateful he wasn't alone. Because of the angels and relatives, he had completely lost his fear of dying. I know Ray and George simply took Gerald by his hand, held him close and carried him away.

More than 250 people attended his funeral service. It was so heartwarming to see that many people pay their respects. It may sound odd, but I felt so proud of my son that day.

Gerald's illness taught me so much about life. I learned that you have to let the people you love know it. You must put your love into words they can carry in their hearts. Gerald never held anger or nursed a grudge against anyone. He taught me how much better life can be once you let your anger go. He also taught me to find joy in giving and doing for others. I had to work hard to develop this way of thinking and being, but it has been worth it, especially considering how people have responded. Just simple human kindness and caring can make a dramatic change in relationships. Gerald never worried about dying. He worried about the lives of the people he loved.

Gerald's Contacts

Naturally, with all that went on before Gerald's death, I certainly wasn't closed minded about after death contacts. Two months after he left, I had one of those dreams that is more than just a dream. I had been praying for a sign that Gerald was okay and my prayers were finally answered in a dramatic way. When he was younger and healthy, Gerald's habit had been to knock on my bedroom door in the morning, then come inside to chat. Well, this is exactly what happened in my dream. He knocked, walked through the door big as life, and said, "Good morning, Mommy!"

"Sweetie, I thought you were dead," I said, startled.

"I am, Mommy, but I had to come and tell you I'm alright so you won't hurt so much."

I stood up and asked, "Can I hug you?"

He just kind of laughed and said, "Well, that's the second reason I'm here. To give you the biggest hug ever." We embraced. I felt his body warm and strong, just as I had when he was alive. While we hugged, he whispered in my ear, "Remember, I am fine. Okay, Mommy?" I opened my eyes and he was gone. Fully awake, I could still sense the pressure of his body against mine where we had touched.

– Susie LeMaster

Connie Vocale and Susie LeMaster learned wonderful life lessons and found peace and healing through contact with their lost children. For Michele DeGennaro, the messages from her lost child and lessons to be learned are vague and shrouded in mystery. Rather than helping her cope, the

contacts she experienced have brought confusion and addi-
tional sadness. Hopefully, with the passing of time and
continued contact, things will become clearer for her. Yet,
as her story reveals, even the most heartbreaking of losses
can bring about hope for the future.

Anthony was our only child. He was born with a blockage in his main bile duct from his liver. Although it was corrected by surgery, the bile that backed up into his liver left him with cirrhosis. Even so, he lived a normal, active life. He loved sports, played Little League baseball, enjoyed football in the snow and, at twelve, developed a passion for golf. He was also an accomplished artist and was looking forward to a career in that field.

My son enjoyed his life immensely. He was always on the go, traveling here and there. When he was old enough to drive that naturally expanded his horizons further. He loved his little car and spent his time zipping all over town, meeting friends, flirting with girls and working at a pizza parlor.

On the outside, everything was great. On the inside, that glitch at his birth became a ticking time bomb. His spleen enlarged, destroying more critical blood cells. His liver grew hard, which made it difficult for blood to pass through it. When he was fifteen, he was put on a transplant list. In the complicated world of transplants, we were informed that he was too healthy at the time for a transplant. He had to get a lot sicker before he would be moved up on the waiting list!

When Anthony was seventeen, an infection destroyed what remained of his liver. He was now sick enough—dramatically so. It's hard to explain the agony a parent endures while her child waits for an organ to become available. Our wait took seven agonizing weeks. Through it all, Anthony never complained. He was very courageous.

When the doctors opened his abdomen up for the transplant, they discovered his condition was far worse than they anticipated. What was scheduled to be a four-hour operation turned into a twelve-hour ordeal. His blood refused to flow to the new liver and it was quickly destroyed as well. A second liver was put in four days later. The rest of his body couldn't handle the stress and Anthony's heart gave out as they were sewing him up.

My son had lost the battle.

Anthony's Contacts

A month or so after Anthony's death, I had the strangest dream. I was walking up a long, winding staircase with an iron rod railing. I was surrounded by white. I heard a woman talking in the distance. I looked down and saw an old lady in a long white robe with a cord tied at the waist. "The tiger is here. He does not want to join our group," she said. I continued to stare at her as I walked higher up the stairs. "The tiger is here. He does not want to join us," she repeated. I had no idea what she meant.

The next thing I knew, a short, balding man was walking beside me. "Your son wants you to know he's happy. He doesn't want you to worry about him."

"Let me talk to Anthony," I asked.

"He doesn't want you to worry about him. He is happy."

"Why can't he tell me himself?" I wondered.

The man looked up, paused, then spoke softly. "Anthony says that when you feel a gentle breeze upon your face, it's him blowing you a kiss." With that, the man was gone.

I woke up with this weird dream spinning in my head. It seemed so real, unlike any dream I'd ever had before. I couldn't go back to sleep. The images and the old lady's words, "The tiger is here. He does not want to join us," kept playing over and over in my mind. Anthony had loved cats. In fact, he owned two when he died. After much thought, I became pretty sure Anthony was the tiger to whom the woman was referring.

A few weeks later, I had a similar dream. An old friend of my father's was standing in front of me. He was a man I knew as a child, but had not seen for decades. I was aware in the dream that he had died twelve years before. It was foggy all around us, as if we were up in the clouds. My dad's friend was wearing a suit, but his lower legs were hidden in the mist. He told me that Anthony was happy and that I didn't need to worry so much about him. He also explained that he was the man by the staircase in the previous dream. Once again, Anthony was not in this dream.

As time passed, Anthony finally appeared to me—but only for brief, odd moments. When I dream about totally unrelated things, Anthony will often appear out of nowhere, walk by, say "hi," give me a hug or kiss, then walk away. After the interruption, the dreams always continue as if nothing has happened. I find these dream contacts strange and a little disturbing. I hope that changes. At least I'm starting to feel that Anthony is happy, wherever he is.

                                        – Michele Degennaro

If the contact from a lost child doesn't help the parent heal, it may be because the parent is approaching the grieving process with the wrong attitude. As Jane Johnson suggests in the next story, parents should embrace their grief, not fight it. They must go through all the stages of the grief process to get to the other side where they will find peace and healing. This openness, combined with an openness to receiving messages from their lost children, helps in the healing process.

My son, Bryan, was always a sweet, understanding guy. He got along with everyone and acted as a peacemaker.

He had a great sense of humor and could make people laugh at themselves or their situation, no matter how hard they tried not to. He loved to fish, race his dirt bike and spend time with his many friends.

He was just starting a new semester at college in Connecticut in September 1995 when he began feeling ill. The glands in his neck had become swollen and his gums started to bleed. Alarmed, he went to the campus medical center. They took his blood, did some tests, then a nurse phoned me. Out of the blue, I was told that my son had leukemia and needed to immediately report to a hospital emergency room. That shocking call launched my family on an emotional roller-coaster ride of fear, despair, hope and trauma, while at the same time kicking off a desperate battle against this terrible disease.

From that moment on, "Bry's" life became so difficult. He spent most of the next fifteen months in the hospital. He developed Bell's Palsy and was unable to eat, drink or swallow on his own. If that wasn't bad enough, he had a severe reaction to one of the chemotherapy drugs and suffered nerve damage and excruciating pain. Unwilling to throw in the towel, he courageously fought his way back from this period of great illness, going from a bed, to a wheel chair, to a walker, then a cane. For a brief period during the summer of 1996, he was allowed to come home. This was a joy for all of us. Knowing what he'd been through and what might lie ahead, he really made the most out of that summer.

The following October, Bry had a relapse that affected his central nervous system while he was awaiting a bone marrow transplant. He battled on, but it was clear that he was sinking fast. Christmas '96 marked the second in a row that he spent in a hospital. We decorated his room by putting Bugs Bunny stickers on the window—he loved Bugs—and hanging Christmas ornaments on his intravenous pole.

Friends and family visited him in shifts, making sure he was never alone very long.

We tried to put on happy faces, but we could see what was happening. The chemotherapy and radiation treatments weakened him to the point where simply opening his Christmas presents wore him out. His body became vulnerable to infections. Sure enough, he developed a severe fever and had to be moved to the intensive care unit. The hospital staff was kind enough to allow us to spend all night with him on New Year's Eve.

On January 2, I received a call from the hospital informing me that they had a "problem." Bry's heart stopped. They were able to resuscitate him, but wanted me to come in. When I walked into his room, I was shocked to see that his neck and face were swollen and his color was awful. "He's dying," the nurse said. "We don't have much time."

I sat down beside the bed and took his hand. His sister was on the opposite side holding his other hand. His cousin lingered at the foot of the bed, while the hospital chaplain stood beside me. Bry's heart stopped again. Literally and figuratively, we just let him go.

I've had many losses in my life and I've spoken with many other heartbroken people. I know from experience that losing a child is the worst thing that can happen to a parent. Watching the child suffer while not being able to save him or ease the pain is pure agony. Such an experience is by far the ultimate emotional pain and torture that a person can go through. The anguish is so great, the reality so objectionable, that the mourning becomes a very, very long process. In truth, a parent never fully recovers. It changes him or her forever.

Everyone must find his or her own path through the grieving process. I've discovered things along the way that have given me help in coping. Talking with and E-mailing other bereaved parents has been critical in my emotional recovery. There is a special comfort in sharing your devastation with people who know so deeply from their own firsthand experiences how you feel. Those lucky enough to have never experienced the loss of a child cannot possibly understand how we suffer.

To occupy my mind, I've been working on an unusual memorial project. It's a fishing area on the shore of Bry's favorite stream that is accessible to the physically challenged. Bry was most at peace when he was fishing, so this is something I know he'd want to share with those who are valiantly struggling to overcome handicaps.

I've also kept a journal. I've learned it can be healing to write down your feelings. Small things, like the warm glow of a candle, can do wonders for the spirit as well.

I cry when the need arises—which is often. It's a natural release which seems to be helpful. Trying to avoid one's pain or numb oneself is foolish and dangerous. There's simply no way around grief. You must go through it and crying is a large part of the process; it really helps. Creative endeavors can be good, too—painting, gardening, cooking—anything that occupies your mind and channels your energy into a productive activity. I try to remember to take care of myself. Fresh flowers, a walk in the woods, reading or long weekend trips all provide temporary relief from the constant reminders of my loss.

In cases like mine, when a child dies from a long, drawn out illness, it's vital to go back in your mind to the better times, to the time before the disease struck. I find myself thinking of Bry's gorgeous smile and recalling the sound of his infectious laugh when he was strong and healthy. I pore over his photos, spend time in his room, fish at his favorite spots and listen to music that we both liked. I celebrate his life—not his illness or his death.

It's been my experience that many parents who have lost children find themselves reassessing their spiritual beliefs. For me, the knowledge that Bry still "is," that he exists in another form, is the only thing that gives me true peace.

Bryan's Contacts

Bryan had a knack for electronics. He wired the phones and television cables in my house and helped others as well. That's why I think he's contacted me through these means. A few weeks after he died, I went with my boyfriend to his house to collect some of Bry's things. My boyfriend had basically moved in with me, so Bryan had stayed at my boyfriend's old place on occasion. On our way back home, the car phone rang with an usual tone that I'd never heard before. When I picked it up, no one was there. A few minutes later, it rang again with the same odd tone. Again, no one was on the other end. Wrong numbers are common, but not so much on car phones. The strange thing was that only three people had that number—my boyfriend who was with me at the time, my daughter and Bryan. My daughter later told me that she hadn't called. In my mind, that left one possible person: Bryan.

Next, the phone by Bryan's old bed in my house began making odd sounds. The first time was when I was sitting on his bed writing the eulogy for his funeral. I read it out loud to get a feel for how it sounded. The moment I finished, the phone buzzed. It wasn't ringing and it wasn't off the hook. In fact, I had never heard a buzzing sound like that from that particular phone or any phone in my life. I repeated the reading and the same strange buzz greeted me at the end. It was as if Bry was giving the eulogy I wrote his approval.

As I've said, fishing was my son's major love, so it wasn't surprising that he appeared to me in the most powerful way during a vivid dream I had about fishing. I was at the lake peering into the water when this huge, very beautiful, gold and peach colored fish cruised by. I saw Bry up on the shore getting out of a boat, so I waved to him. "Bry, come quick! Look at this big fish!" He walked over and knelt beside me, his body right up close to mine. His face appeared different, larger, kind of "heavenly" and seemed to hover over me. He was wearing the most gentle, loving expression.

"Yes, Ma, nice fish. But more important, my beloved mother!" he said, giving me a kiss. When I woke up, I felt calm inside, more centered and solid.

Another dream involved butterflies, which I've since learned is a common phenomena among bereaved parents. In my dream, all these butterflies were flying around. I noticed that one had not yet fully transformed from the caterpillar stage. It seemed to be struggling to do so. Looking closer, I realized that it was badly injured. I became very worried that it wouldn't be able to complete it's magical metamorphosis into a beautiful winged creature. Suddenly, to my surprise and relief, it became a stunning butterfly that was larger and more colorful than all the others. It had these filmy orange and pink wings that were just gorgeous. Unfortunately, my joy soon turned to despair and frustration. As quickly as it sprang forth, it perished. In the dream, I began explaining what happened to the creature to a stranger who was standing next to me. "Don't you see," the stranger responded. "It was just at the brink of spreading it's wings in full beauty and then it died. Just like Bryan."

When I woke up, though the image of the butterfly's death and the stranger's statement were seemingly negative, they ironically had the opposite effect upon me. I was actually comforted.

Bryan was a beautiful, dear person. In his short life, he had grown into a wise and wonderful man. He touched many lives in profound and positive ways. He loved and was loved. He achieved the things that are really important in life.

Unlike the butterfly in the dream whose life was almost instantly snatched away, he was able to soar for a little while.

– Jane Johnson

Again and again, the stories told by parents show that the pain of losing their children to illness is ultimately transformed to peace through after death contacts. While society expects parents to "bounce back" after several months, the pain and grief may last for years or a lifetime. However, with assuring contacts from the beyond, parents' heartwrenching pain can subside, knowing their children are healthy and happy in the afterlife. This is especially important for parents of children lost to senseless violence, as the stories in the next chapter illustrate.

Chapter Five

Senseless Deaths, Peaceful Signs

Though a child's death always leaves bereft parents wondering why, when an act of violence takes a child's life, it is especially difficult to bear the loss, for the parents must cope with grief and sadness plus all the anger and mixed emotions that come about when they learn that another person willfully and purposefully took their child's life. The pain is compounded all the more when the grief process is dragged out by endless legal proceedings.

As the next stories show, the aftermath of such senseless deaths can be overwhelming. The intense emotions created by these violent deaths can be so crushing that many of the anguished parents left behind only find comfort when the departed return to give them messages of hope.

Mike came into the world fighting like a bear. I was in labor for forty-four hours and still couldn't get the ten pound, twenty-three inch, breech baby to turn around and get into the proper position. The doctors finally had to do a caesarean section. My son had what is now known as ADHD (attention deficit hyperactivity disorder) and thus had a hard time in school. He also had trouble dealing with authority.

However, he rarely troubled me, because he was so warm and affectionate—both as a boy and as a grown-up. We did battle once in a while, especially in his teenage years, but he was usually loving and always saw me as his "mommy."

My son used to give me the most wonderful Mother's Day presents. Whether it was something he bought or made himself, I cherished them all. One of my favorites is a gold bracelet that says "I love you mom." I never take it off.

When he was in his late teens, I helped him get a job at the company where I worked. To show his gratitude, he used his entire first paycheck to buy me a special present. The way he presented the gift gave me real joy. He came home and handed me a paper bag. I felt something move at the bottom and quickly tossed the bag right back to him. I'm no shrinking violet when it comes to animals. I love pets and have a house full of them. The problem was, Mike had been talking about buying a snake and that's where I drew the line. I thought he was trying to scare me, so no matter how much he tried to get me to open the bag, I refused. He finally opened it for me and pulled out a beautiful, snow white baby cockatiel. That was the kind of person Mike was—playful, teasing, kind and generous.

Shortly before Mike's twentieth birthday, he disappeared. He was last seen with his friend Dave in Dave's car. I called the police to report him missing when he never returned. They subsequently found Dave's vehicle in a bad part of town stripped of everything valuable. The day after I reported Mike missing, I received a call that shattered my life. It was a neighbor checking to see if my son had come home yet. When I told my neighbor that Mike had not returned yet, he said, "Eileen, you had better sit down, because I have a horrible story to tell."

He told me that his nephew had been to a party the night before. A boy there was bragging to all who would listen that he and a friend had shot and killed Mike and Dave and left their bodies in a cow pasture. I immediately called the police. They tried to convince me that it was probably "just a story" and advised me to ignore it. I knew in my soul that this was not "just a story" and I became hysterical. They finally agreed to send someone to my house. When the officers arrived, they interviewed my neighbor's nephew. He must have been very convincing, because after that, the police took the "story" very seriously.

The police called for a helicopter and searched a field beyond a wooded area near my house. I sat on my front lawn crying as I watched them hunt for my son's body. I knew when the helicopter landed in the field and the police cars started swarming in that the story was true. And indeed, the police found them. Instead of planning a birthday party for a vibrant young man, I had to plan a funeral. That was the beginning of the nightmare.

Many different stories were told about what exactly happened in the field where my son was found. Basically, it came down to this: Mike and his friend were lured to the field by two teens on the pretense of doing some target shooting. The night before, one of the teens had shot a man during a drug deal gone bad and was desperately on the run from the police. He and the other teen planned to rob Mike and Dave and steal Dave's car. Something must have gone wrong or there was a change of plan. Dave was shot in the head and in the scuffle Mike tried to run away but tripped and was shot twice in the head as well. The two teens were later taken into custody by the police. Each one immediately fingered the other as the shooter.

For me, the pain that followed was almost too much to bear. There are absolutely no words to describe it. If anyone had ever tried to convince me a person could feel that kind of anguish and live through it, I would have called him a liar. Life seemed so unfair. Mothers aren't supposed to bury their children. We are supposed to die first! I thought about Mike from the moment I opened my eyes in the morning until I fell asleep at night. Did he call out my name? Did he want his mom? Every time I closed my eyes, all I could see was my son running for his life, falling, crawling on his hands and knees, begging to be spared. This image replayed itself over and over in my mind. I was in such a fog that I ran through red lights without realizing it. To this day, I can't remember anything about the week after he was murdered.

More than 300 people—mostly teenagers—attended Mike's funeral. "I've never seen so many people gathered around a funeral home, young and beautiful people, gathered for compassion, love and friendship," said the rector of St. Ignatius Church. I used to look at those same teenagers and see earrings, shaved heads, long hair and think they were no good. But they turned out to be wonderful people with hearts of gold. Without the help of my family, friends, the community and Mike's young friends, I wouldn't have made it through the painful ordeal.

Just as I was beginning to heal, the murder trials began. I now had to face the boys who were responsible for taking my son's life. Being in the courtroom was pure hell. The judge warned us—friends and family alike—not to show any emotion or cause any disruptions or we would be expelled. It seemed unfair to me to expect family and friends not to show any emotion when lawyers and the defendants were discussing in detail how Mike suffered before he died. We were made to feel victimized over and over again. It seemed as if the criminals had all the rights and we had none.

One of the teens was convicted and sentenced to two consecutive life terms without parole. He avoided the death penalty by agreeing to testify against the other boy. He later reneged on the deal and went mute. Despite that, the judge refused to change his sentence. The teen's testimony was critical to the case against the second boy and his change of heart resulted in the second teen walking away a free man. He now lives two miles from our house.

It was all so hard to accept. These two teens were not only responsible for ending Mike and Dave's lives, they destroyed our lives, the lives of their families and, in the case of the boy who got two life sentences, he destroyed his own life as well.

Everyone kept telling me how strong I was and how proud they were of me. If they had only known the terrible thoughts of vengeance that went through my head, they probably wouldn't have been so complimentary.

My son was very popular and had scores of friends. In the ensuing months, those kids didn't drift away as people tend to do in these situations. They kept me going. My family and Mike's friends became my lifeline. They were at my house every day telling me how much they loved me. They gave me the hugs, comfort and support that got me through the tough moments. They called me at work to cheer me up, took me bowling, treated me to dinners and even brought me to one of their parties. Without their support, I might have lost my mind. I love each and every one of those young men and women with all my heart. I often say that I lost a son, but gained fifty children.

Mike's friends constructed a makeshift memorial near the place where he and Dave were murdered. They built a white cross, stitched a needlepoint tapestry which reads "We love you and miss you," wrote messages on concrete blocks, hung an American flag, displayed empty bottles of the boys favorite soft drinks and even propped their surfboards against a fence. They frequently held candlelight vigils there. When the Florida sun and wet weather eventually eroded most of it, they organized a car wash and other fund-raisers in order to finance a permanent memorial. The kids made enough money to purchase a headstone with both boys' pictures on it and had a bench made with "In Loving Memory of Mike and Dave" etched on it. They also planted an oak tree for shade and paid to have the area beautifully landscaped. Best of all, they haven't left it at that. Every time I go to the memorial, I usually find someone already there saying hello to Mike and Dave. I often find letters, jewelry, cards, stuffed animals, toys, flowers, hats and other sentimental items placed there from the night before. To know my son and his friend were loved to that extent is such a blessing.

Their efforts have been extraordinarily comforting, because no parent wants their child to be forgotten. That is the biggest fear I have. Thanks to the Internet, I was able to put up a Web page dedicated to my wonderful son, Michael Robert Tiedt, which serves as a memorial of his life. My recommendation to any other parents who have lost a child to murder is to please, please, reach out for help. Only another parent whose child has been taken away by violence can truly understand the particular sort of pain that comes with such a loss.

Mike's Contacts

For the first eight months after Mike was murdered, my daughter, Taya, often came into my bed in the middle of the night. She was sixteen at the time, so this was not typical behavior for her. She told me that Mike kept waking her up by getting in bed with her. She said she could feel him crawl in and lay down beside her. She slept on a waterbed, so the movement of another body was unmistakable. She could even see the indentation of his body in the mattress. The bed is up against a wall, so anyone getting in over her would have to get in exactly as she described.

She also came into my room screaming that she felt bugs crawling on her face. Only there were never any bugs to be found. Disturbed by these events, we went to a psychic who told us that the "bugs" Taya felt were really caused by Mike tickling her with her long hair. We both gasped in amazement, because that's the exact way Mike used to wake his sister up when he was alive!

Although Taya was unnerved by what was going on, I found it comforting to know that Mike was still around. I wasn't really surprised that he made contact the way he did; there was never anything subtle about Mike! Since then, I always assure parents who have contact with their departed children that they're not crazy, but blessed and lucky. I tell them, "This is your chance. Reach out to your son or daughter."

– Eileen LaCasse

Murder is always senseless to the family, friends and parents of the victim. Facing her own child's death and the mothers of the boys who took her son's life were both very painful experiences for Judi Walker. It was only through the support of friends and loved ones, as well as the miracle of her son's ongoing presence in her life, that she was able to get through the ordeal.

Shane was my first child. Right from the beginning, December 3, 1977, he was a wonderful baby. Through the years, brother, husband, father and friend were added to his many attributes. He was friendly, outgoing, had a large circle of friends and was always willing to drop anything to help a pal in need even if it meant missing out on his favorite activities like hunting, fishing, playing baseball and driving his truck.

My husband and I were very proud of him. He wasn't perfect, but he never gave us much trouble. We had our ups and downs like all families, but he knew we loved him and we knew he loved us. He was free to talk to us about anything. We were always there for him.

Shane's younger sisters, Jennie and Laurie, cherished him as well. Unlike so many teenage boys, he actually talked to his sisters and listened to them. He took the time to be with them and made an effort to take them places and do things with them. He told me that he was looking forward to the time they were old enough to date so he could give their boyfriends a hard time.

Shane married in his late teens, worked for a pizza restaurant and had a pair of beautiful twin daughters—Krista and Kristen. They were the light of his life and they adored their daddy.

On October 27, 1997, at 9:05 P.M., Shane rode with a friend to a local ballpark. They were familiar with the area because Shane had played baseball there since he was five. They parked and began talking to another youth standing outside the car. A second boy, who had had a dispute with Shane's friend, ran up to the passenger side. He pulled out a shotgun and stuck it into the window, aiming it at Shane's friend. The friend tried to open his car door and escape. Somehow, in the confusion, the gun went off, hitting Shane in the face. My son died instantly. He was nineteen years old.

The two boys outside the car, and a third who was part of the planned shooting, were all captured by the police within a few hours. They reiterated that their argument was with Shane's friend, that they had no idea that Shane would be in the car that evening and that his death was unintentional.

Their claims gave me little comfort. My son was gone. To add to my pain, I had to endure the endless legal ordeal that followed. There were hearings, motions, pre-trial motions and court appearance after court appearance, each one bringing back all the horrible memories. I hated them, because I didn't understand the reason for them. It was so difficult to go downtown and see the boys who ended my son's life. Yet, to ensure that justice was served, I went to the courthouse everyday and was forced to spend time in the gallery and hallways with the defendants' mothers and families. It was emotionally overwhelming.

Though I wanted to hate the boys and their families, their mothers turned out to be very caring and compassionate ladies who were dealing with their own pain. They were very kind to me and even tried to befriend me. I appreciated their compassion and was able to overcome my anger towards them, but I just couldn't develop a friendship with the mothers of the boys who killed my son. I didn't hold what their sons did against them. We can't help what our children do. But I feel that to be friends with someone—especially a parent—I have to care about their families and their children and I didn't want to care about their sons. I wanted their sons punished! I couldn't forget that despite the trouble their sons were in, those parents at least got to see their children everyday in court, while I would never get to see Shane again.

I was in a store one day when I saw one defendant's mother. She approached me and we started talking about the court proceedings. Another woman heard us and asked if we were talking about the Hebert murder. When we both said yes, she responded that it was horrible and that Shane was such a good boy. "Those three who killed him should get the death penalty!" she spat. Despite my own feelings, I was horrified for the other mother. I walked away without saying a word.

After a while, I just wanted it all to be over. As the months passed, I couldn't understand why the court proceedings had to keep dragging on and on. It was torture.

The more legal proceedings I went through, the worse it became. Each time I saw my son's murderers it ripped me apart. I started to shake just thinking about it. I became so unglued emotionally that, at one point, I couldn't even leave the house to go to the proceedings or anywhere else. My heart started pounding, I had trouble breathing and my body convulsed. I was terrified of being out in the world.

Finally, the courtroom drama came to a close. Two of the three young men pleaded guilty to armed robbery and each received a fifteen-year prison sentence. The third, the alleged "triggerman" rejected all plea bargains and went to trial. He was found not guilty. Apparently, because of the number of perpetrators involved, the jury was unable to decide "beyond a reasonable doubt" which person actually fired the gun.

With time, I've been able to work through my anger and sadness and let go of the things I can't change. Instead of being filled with those negative thoughts and feelings, I think of Shane with fondness and love. He taught me a lot about life, even though I was the parent and he was the child. He showed me how to love completely and unconditionally in life and he continues to teach me even in death. He has shown me that I have the strength to pick up the pieces, withstand a broken heart and go on living.

Shane's Contacts

On December 9, 1997, about six weeks after Shane was murdered, my husband and I were in our van when all of a sudden Shane's face appeared in front of me. It was clear as day. He said, "I'm cool. I'm cool. I'm really, really cool." When I tried to reach out and touch him, he was gone.

Three weeks later, he came back again. I was sitting one afternoon at the computer when my eight-year-old daughter brought me a picture of a rainbow she had drawn. She asked me to write a poem about Shane to go with her drawing, because rainbows reminded her of Shane. I wasn't in the mood at the moment and put the picture aside. She was very disappointed. All of a sudden, the lights on the computer blinked on and off and the machine shut down. There wasn't a storm at the time and when I checked the wires and plugs, everything appeared to be in order. Then I noticed some kind of golden light shining in through the patio door. My daughters and I went outside to see what it was. We looked up and there, across the sky, was the biggest, most beautiful rainbow we had ever seen. The rainbow was so bright it gave the tops of the trees a golden glow. After a while, it started to fade. When it was almost gone, my daughter, using one of Shane's nicknames, said, "Bubba, please come back!" Suddenly, the rainbow returned as bright as before. Convinced that Shane was sending a message, I immediately went inside and wrote the poem to go with my daughter's rainbow drawing.

Shane came to me for the third time a few months later. I had long before stitched a design of two squirrels on a long panel for my husband. Shane loved it and asked me for years to make him something similar. I had been in the process of creating a similar panel for his Christmas present when he was killed. It was going to be a surprise, so he never knew I was making it for him. After he was killed, I put the panel away half-finished. I couldn't touch it or look at it, because seeing it made me cry. The following March, I was writing in my journal about the guilt I felt never finishing the panel. I wrote that I was determined to complete the stitching one day and do something special with it. As soon as I finished writing those words, I heard Shane's voice in my head say, *Okay, give it to Peter.* Peter was one of Shane's best friends. It was odd, because I would have never thought to give Peter the artwork. The next day, Peter came over for a surprise visit. While there, he mentioned to me that he was bothered by the fact that he had nothing of Shane's to remember him by. I was stunned. I told him about the panel I was stitching and what Shane had told me to do with it. I promised to give Peter the panel when it was complete. Then I went to the closet, retrieved the panel and showed it to Peter. We were both so moved seeing it that we cried together. It was the first time since the night Shane died that I had been able to even touch the piece. I started working on it that evening. I felt my guilt and pain slowly dissipate. In a few days, I finished the embroidery and gave it to his friend as Shane had requested.

– Judi Walker

As the various stories have shown, contact with a murdered child brings most parents comfort and healing and comes in many forms. Through tragedy comes supernatural expressions of love. Few contacts, however, are as unusual as the one in the next story.

Joshua was our only child. He brought such joy to our lives! There was never a dull moment raising a spirited boy who was always on the go. His dad worked long hours so that we wouldn't have to put Josh in daycare and I could spend all my time with him. We spent many hours together just playing and exploring the world. He especially loved riding the Metro bus to the mall and watching the ice skaters.

His toddler years flew by. Soon he was off to school, making his own circle of friends. He trusted everyone and didn't believe that anyone should be a stranger. His philosophy was that if a person talked to him, he or she must be a friend. Even though Josh and I spent less time together when he went off to school, our bond remained just as strong as when he was little.

During his pre-teen years, the practical joker in Josh emerged. He was always pulling some kind of harmless prank on someone. He loved to make people laugh. More importantly, Josh knew how far to push things and when to stop. He was generous and kind as well as mischievous. He could be a real stinker if you were his target, but it was always done in fun.

When Josh was thirteen, the violence and gang activity that plagued the larger cities south of us began to spread to our town. We decided to move from California and take Josh as far away from the violence as we could. We chose a small, rural town in central Missouri where we thought he would be safe.

Josh grew into fine young man. When he graduated high school, he joined the army. That turned out to be a mistake. It didn't take him long to realize the military life wasn't for him. He hated guns and explosives. He often called from the base at Fort Polk, Louisiana, lamenting his fate. "Mom, I hate it here! I don't like these live fire exercises. I'm afraid someone will shoot me. Some of these guys don't know how to handle guns. I want to come home!"

He endured it for five months, arranged an honorable discharge and happily returned to Missouri. On the day he came home, he walked into the house and announced, "Mom, I'm home!" as if he'd never left. His voice was music to my ears. It was so wonderful to have the noise and activity of a young person around the house again. He found a job, enrolled in college and set out on a new course that was as un-military as you can get—he decided to become an art teacher.

Two weeks later, Josh stopped at a nearby friend's house to introduce his new girlfriend to his friends before bringing her home to meet his parents. At the same time he was there, I became anxious and had an awful feeling that something terrible was going to happen. My body became cold; I was nearly paralyzed with fear and I soon became sick to my stomach.

Down the road, unbeknownst to me, Josh's friend had put on a warrior's mask and was playing around with a six-teen gauge shotgun. He jokingly pointed it at various people there, then turned it on Josh's new girlfriend. Josh, uncomfortable around guns, stood in front of his girlfriend to shield her. The boy pointed the gun at Josh's chest. Josh asked, "Is the gun loaded?" His friend said, "Let's find out," and pulled the trigger.

The gun was loaded.

In a flash, because of some foolish horseplay, a dream ended, a golden heart stopped beating and a family was destroyed. The "juvenile offender" who killed my eighteen-year-old son served a few months in detention, then was released with a clean record.

Josh had walked out our door that day beaming so brightly. How could I have known that he'd never walk back into our house again? How could I have known that would be the last time I would see his beautiful face? That last image is etched in my mind forever. I still can see my beloved boy standing at the head of the stairs, his bright blue eyes shining, his smile radiating. It's the last thing I see at night and the first thing I see each morning. In between is pain—the most incredible pain imaginable. I'm learning to live with it, but even years later it's still fresh and raw.

At the two year anniversary of Joshua's death, I calculated that it had been 730 days, 17,520 hours, and 1,051,200 minutes since I last saw my son's smile, or heard him say "Hey Mom...I love you!"

Josh's Contacts

Three weeks after Josh's death, I went for a drive just to get out of the house. I drove through a park where Josh used to hang out with his friends and once I started, I couldn't stop crying. Out of the corners of my blurry eyes, I saw him sitting in the seat next to me. It was only for a brief moment, but it was clearly Josh.

I didn't hear or see Josh again for the next twelve months. I used to call Josh "Bear," so my husband bought me a little talking bear that he thought might be comforting. When I squeezed the stuffed animal's tummy, it said "I am your guardian angel. I am your special friend." I placed it on the windowsill in our bedroom. On New Year's Day, I was in the adjacent bathroom brushing my hair and was moved to call out, "Happy New Year, Bear!" From the bedroom, I heard the bear respond, "I am your guardian angel. I am your special friend." It startled me. Not sure of what I'd heard, I walked into the bedroom, stood by the window and looked up at the bear.

"Josh, was that you?" I asked. The bear answered, "I am your guardian angel. I am your special friend." Excited, I started talking to the bear as if it was Josh. Every time I addressed it, the bear spoke. I hesitated in bringing it to my husband's attention, because he didn't believe in any kind of paranormal occurrences, but I felt sure he couldn't deny that something miraculous was happening. I finally called him into the bedroom. "Josh, tell Dad Happy New Year." We waited a few minutes, but the bear said nothing. I felt very foolish, but just as we started to leave the room, the bear spoke. My husband was so stunned he bumped into me. Tears came to his eyes. "What did you do?" he asked me. I was standing right next to him, so he knew I hadn't been touching the toy. The bear then spoke again. Now my husband was convinced.

"Happy New Year, son," my husband said. The bear responded to that as well.

Following that incident, the little bear was silent for months. Then one night we had a terrible storm. Lightning flashed in the sky and thunder rocked the house. Storms like that always terrified Josh. Suddenly, the bear started repeating its phrases really fast over and over like it was nervous and frightened. I got up and brought it to bed with me, cuddled it and spoke soothingly, assuring the bear that everything would be all right. The bear's voice slowed, then stopped, like a child falling asleep in its mother's arms.

For several days after that, the little bear spoke to us just as we were going to bed. It repeated its lines for a few minutes and then stopped. One night it went on longer than usual. My husband, exhausted and unnerved from a bad day at work, became irritated and said "Okay, Josh, that's enough. I need to get some sleep, so knock it off!"

The bear has never spoken again.

– Monika Hedglin

Sometimes, parents don't even get a chance to grieve for their dead child. Instead, they have to put all their thoughts and energy into fighting for justice when the system fails. In the next story, not only did the parents bring their son's killer to justice, they helped to change the system from within and through that effort, found peace.

Brian was the youngest of my three children. He had a typical childhood, spending his summers playing Little League baseball and most of the year studying nature and earning merit badges with the Cub Scouts and Boy Scouts. He was an average student who preferred working with his hands, especially in the field of auto mechanics. After graduating high school, he took a position at furniture store as a stock room supervisor and was planning to enroll in a technical school.

On the evening of Saturday, June 24, 1989—almost two months after his nineteenth birthday—Brian left the house to go out with a friend. I really didn't want my son to hang out with this person, because I had a bad feeling about him. He seemed phony to me and was bad tempered. Brian gave me a hug and a kiss, assuring me he would be okay. "Don't worry, Mom," he said with a smile. "I'll be home early. I love you!"

During the course of the evening, his friend needed money for gas and asked Brian to cover it. My son refused. An argument ensued. Brian's "friend" picked up some kind of heavy object and proceeded to viciously bludgeon him to death. The crazed youth took Brian's wallet, then dumped his ravaged body in a junk yard. A worker discovered the body the next morning. Half the head was gone. We later learned that the friend had had a violent argument with his girlfriend earlier that same night and she feared he was going to kill her. The girlfriend had been a long time friend of Brian's, so it's possible the two young men also argued over the way the violent young man treated her.

My son's killer walked the streets for the next eighteen months, because the police didn't have enough evidence to arrest him. He covered his tracks well, washing his clothes and car and discarding Brian's wallet. He was so demented and arrogant that he sometimes sat across the street from our house, laughing and taunting us as we came and went. Unwilling to play the roles of helpless victims, my husband and I went public with our story and soon became this boy's biggest nightmare. We found out and kept track of where he worked, where he lived and what car he drove despite numerous changes. We also learned he was driving without a license or insurance, so we called the police on him whenever we saw him in his car. In addition, we acquired his "secret" juvenile criminal record and passed it out to the media. I risked being arrested for that, but I didn't care, so long as my actions might lead to this man's arrest.

On the first anniversary of Brian's death, we held a memorial service followed by a press conference. We reminded the media that we knew who killed our son. I said, "I will go to my grave working to put Brian's murderer behind bars and keep him there." The media was very sympathetic to our plight and helped to put additional pressure on the police to step up the now stalled investigation.

The young man finally slipped up. He got drunk one night and bragged to a new girlfriend about the murder. She fearfully covered for him for a while, but finally broke under repeated police questioning. He was arrested and charged with first degree murder and armed robbery. After a year of waiting to go to trial and after being promised by the District Attorney that there would be no plea-bargain, the defendant was allowed to plead to manslaughter at the last minute. The plea was accepted over our objections. He was sentenced to fifteen to twenty years with parole eligibility after ten years.

Furious, I decided to take matters into my own hands. I wanted to ensure that my son's death would not be in vain. I began lobbying to change the laws that govern the punishment for these crimes, focusing on what I felt were lenient sentences, especially when dealing with juveniles, early paroles and the suppression of past criminal records. I testified on behalf of the Victims Rights Bill, the Juvenile Justice Bill and the Truth and Sentencing Bill, all of which were passed by the Massachusetts State Legislature. I also founded and operated the North Shore Chapter of Parents of Murdered Children and began a Victim-Inmate Prison Program. The latter is an innovative outreach program that brings the relatives of homicide victims in contact with convicted murderers—though not the defendants in their cases. The purpose is to give the inmates an intensely personal understanding of the lingering pain that their anti-social behavior has caused. The experience is usually cathartic for both the family and the offender.

Ironically, it was this unusual program that did the most to initiate my healing process. In the beginning, I wanted all murderers executed and firmly believed in the death penalty. I felt that, if given the opportunity, I wouldn't hesitate to kill my son's murderer with my bare hands. The pain, anguish, hate and need for vengeance can be overwhelming. However, after meeting with these convicts and seeing them as human beings, I changed my mind. Most of the inmates on death row are impoverished minorities. You rarely see a rich, well-connected white man there. I questioned scores of men waiting to die and asked if the death penalty had in any way entered their minds when they committed their crimes. They all told me that it didn't, which led me to believe the death penalty is not a deterrent. I also realized that it wouldn't make me feel any better to see the man who killed my son put to death. That wouldn't accomplish what I wanted the most: to bring Brian back. I still believe murderers should spend their lives in prison, but I've come to believe that no one has the right to take another person's life, not even the government.

I feel so strongly about it that I began speaking out against capital punishment. This led to an emotional appearance before the National Commission Against the Death Penalty in Philadelphia. A documentary was made of this hearing called "Lethal Selection," which is frequently shown around the country, especially at colleges and universities.

I further testified before the State House in Boston, joining many others in an effort that led to the death penalty being defeated by a single vote.

Continuing these activities, I signed on with a national organization called Murder Victims' Families for Reconciliation and was honored to be included in their booklet with other members. I was presented with an award for lobbying on behalf of the Juvenile Justice Bill and received a humanitarian award from the Essex County Sheriff's Department.

Our family also gives out a yearly grant in Brian's memory to a Boy Scout from Troop 61 in Saugus, Massachusetts. We pay to send a youth from that troop to scout camp and place his name on a plaque that hangs in the scout room at the local church. This June will mark the eleventh year that this memorial has been given out.

I truly believe that no matter what happens in our lives, we have a choice to exist either with hate and anger or to create something positive out of horrible tragedies. When Brian was murdered, I prayed to God to show me what he wanted me to do. The answer was social activism. By pouring my time and energy into these grassroots activities, I have found peace in my life.

Brian's Contacts

The night Brian left the house for the last time, I dozed off around midnight and had the strangest dream. We were at Disneyworld on the popular "It's A Small World" ride, which had always been one of Brian's favorites. In the dream, the automated boats stopped and Brian hopped out and walked away from me. Two very beautiful women with long, flowing hair, wearing filmy, white gowns that extended to their ankles, appeared at his side and took him with them. Although it was a peaceful sight, I became sick inside, instinctively picking up on the terrible meaning of what I'd just observed. I sat up in bed and glanced at the clock. It was 1:00 A.M. I looked around the house for Brian, but he had not yet returned home. He never would. Brian's death certificate listed the time of his death as 1:00 A.M.

Did I really see angels escorting Brian to heaven? I believe so. What else could it have been at that precise moment? The dream was so vivid that I often wonder if I was actually there with Brian when the angels took him.

That Sunday, the phone rang at 7:30 A.M. When I answered, I heard nothing but loud static. Then it became strangely quiet. A warm, peaceful feeling bathed over me. Brian's body had been found at 7:30 A.M. My daughter later told me she received an identical call where she was staying. First, she heard loud static, then quiet, then she felt peaceful.

We both wondered if this was Brian trying to tell us he was okay.

Prior to his killer's arrest, Brian's spirit appeared to be extremely restless. A lamp in our living room would snap on and off and when the television was on, the stations would quickly flip by the same way they did when Brian used to channel "surf" when he was agitated. Once in a while, books even came flying out of the bookcase.

Of all the books in my house, only three in particular kept popping out of the bookcase. They all had titles having to do with death, justice and the afterlife. No matter where I put them—and I changed their locations numerous times—they'd always end up across the room on the floor. They never just teetered on the edge of the shelf and fell down. They always shot from the bookcase, landing near the opposite wall.

After the plea agreement, most of the otherworldly events stopped. The only one that has remained on a consistent basis is the channel surfing. On Brian's birthday or his passing anniversary, the channels will invariably start zipping by again. I see this as Brian assuring us that he's still around.

More than five years after the last incident with the books, a new title began launching itself from the shelf. It was called *A Mother's Love*. I believe this was Brian's way of thanking me for all the work I did in helping to identify, capture and convict his killer, along with my numerous campaigns to push through social reforms.

I can't explain how or why these events took place, but I know that they did and I'm glad they did! It gives me peace knowing that Brian's spirit lives on and that he's okay. I don't care who believes me or who doesn't. I just thank God and Brian for all these wonderful signs.

– Phyllis Hotchkiss

*The loss of a child at the hands of a murderer is shocking
and devastating for a parent. Yet the murderer is a tangible
target for blame, guilt and anger. However, seeing a child's
life snuffed out from drug abuse leaves a parent both missing her child and upset with the child for taking such risks.
In addition, the guilt over not doing more to help the child
can be overwhelming for a parent. Yet drug abuse among
young people is a huge problem that many parents have to
face. Unfortunately, as the following story tells, parents
aren't always able to save their children from the addicting
call of drugs.*

My daughter Lisa spent the early part of her life bathed
in happiness. She loved to talk and was always in
motion, climbing, jumping, doing flips, you name it. She was
an upbeat baby and gregarious toddler. If she could have
stayed five years old forever, she would have been perfectly
content.

But her carefree attitude was fleeting. The first signs
of trouble came very early on, before she started her education. She had always eagerly walked with her grandpa while
he escorted our other children to school. However, Lisa
always made it clear it was the walk she loved, not the
prospect of actually attending class. She did not want to go
to school herself and had no intention of ever doing so. Her
grandpa tried to get her accustomed to the inevitability of it.
"When you turn five, you'll be going, too!" he said one afternoon.

"No! When I'm five, I'll just have a baby instead of
going to school!" she insisted. Of course, life doesn't work
that way, so it was off to kindergarten, like it or not. Soon,
she didn't mind school so much, but once again made it clear
to us that the half-day of kindergarten was as far as she ever

intended to progress. She fully planned to be a first grade dropout. "Ohhhhhh nooooooo," she insisted the following year when we tried to take her to her first grade classroom. "I only signed up for kindergarten!"

Again, life doesn't go the way you always want it to, so, much to her extreme dismay, she was forced to attend grammar school. Lisa must have known something we didn't, because right off she started having all kinds of problems. She had what is now known as ADD/HD (attention deficit deficiency and hyperactivity disorder). The idea of sitting still and having to pay attention just wasn't in her make up. Teachers didn't know much about ADD back then, so they instead viewed Lisa as a discipline problem. I feel a lot of guilt over not figuring it out myself and getting her the proper help. However, I also feel that her teachers should have recognized that she was generally a good child and that there was something wrong. They used to scold me that she needed to stop watching so much television and study more, assuming that television was what kept her distracted even in school. I always told them the truth: Lisa hardly watched any television for the same reason that she didn't like doing homework; she couldn't sit still long enough.

Lisa's inherent learning disabilities weren't discovered until she was in the sixth grade. By then, she felt ostracized from other children and her self-esteem was in the gutter. Seeking comfort, she fell into a crowd of misfits and social outcasts. When she reached her teens, she began running away from home on a regular basis. She'd be gone for days at a time. We'd spend the time fearfully wondering if she was dead or alive. Eventually, she'd show up again at home.

It wasn't long before she began trying to deaden her emotional pain with drugs. By her late teens, she had moved out of our home permanently and had become a heroin addict. Clearly she was out of control; I wanted to help her and felt guilty that I couldn't.

When she wanted to return home, I told her she couldn't unless she entered a drug rehabilitation program and cleaned herself up. This was the only way I felt I could help her. Lisa refused and eventually was caught buying drugs by the police and spent eight months in jail. Again, we refused to bail her out unless she made an attempt to change her ways. While we couldn't get her to comply with our wishes, the legal system proved to be more persuasive. On the condition that she go directly into drug rehabilitation, they offered her an early release. She accepted the offer. I let her come home for the two week period before her drug rehabilitation program was to begin.

This brief window of sanity was one of the most wonderful times in our lives with her. She was free of drugs and had returned to being the sweet, funny, happy girl we once knew. She appeared to be serious about staying drug-free and looked forward to successfully completing the rehabilitation program and changing her life. She also knew the consequences of failing. "Don't worry, I won't use again," she assured me. "I know that after you've been clean for a while and then use heroin again, it's easy to overdose and die."

She left our home and began the drug rehabilitation program with a positive attitude, but the lure of the needle proved to be more than Lisa could handle. On August 27, 1998, the police came to our door in the early morning hours and brought us the devastating news. I refused to believe it. My child was in drug rehab—how could she have died? I called the facility and they wouldn't give me any information about Lisa until I told them the police were with me at my house. Then they finally admitted that Lisa had vanished in the middle of the night forty-eight hours earlier.

I had dreaded this moment for a large part of Lisa's life. When she first ran away, I feared that she might become a victim of violence on the streets. When she became an addict, I knew that the drugs themselves or the lifestyle and the people that come with them could lead to her death. Yet, with all the years of preparing for the worst, I wasn't able to handle her death when it actually happened. The whole next year was a blur to me. In my own way, I became as lost as my daughter had been.

Lisa's Contacts

After the funeral, I found myself home alone one evening. My husband, my daughter, Gina, and her daughter, Sonia, who were living with us, were all out. Whenever one of my girls forgot her key, she would stand at the front door and call, "Mama" until I'd hear her and let her in. That night, as I passed the front door, I heard a female voice call, "Mama." I assumed it was Gina.

"Just a minute," I responded. When I opened the door, there was nobody around. I searched the screened porch and outside, but there was no one. Remembering that Gina and Lisa's voices sounded identical, I became certain it was Lisa trying to tell me she was okay.

A month or so later, when my family was at home, we were reminiscing about Lisa, sharing some of our good memories of her. Sonia was especially missing her aunt and feeling very sad. To cheer her up, we reminded Sonia of all the gifts Lisa had given her over the years by which she could remember her aunt. Gina, overcome with emotion, excused herself and went to her room. Moments later, Gina called out to me from her room. "Did you put a pair of earrings on my dresser?" she asked. I called back, "No." Curious, I went to

Gina's room and saw the pair of little bear earrings that she was referring to. Lisa had given the earrings to Sonia some time before. Sonia had lost them and nobody had seen them for months. I'm certain their sudden appearance was a result of our conversation about the gifts Lisa had given Sonia. It was Lisa's way of reminding Sonia about her gift of the adorable earrings and letting us all know she was close by.

One of the most startling and enduring contacts from Lisa involves a small, porcelain angel doll. I have a set of the dolls, which I display in a bookcase in our computer room. One of the angels has long brown hair and delicate features. Everybody who sees the angel doll tells me it looks just like Lisa did when she was a little girl.

One afternoon, I was cleaning the computer room and had just finished straightening the desk that sits across the room from the bookcase where the angel dolls sit. I put the cleaning supplies away and when I returned to the room to use the computer, I was stunned to find that the brown-haired angel that looks like Lisa was no longer on the book-shelf, but was instead sitting right next to the computer! No one was home except me and I certainly hadn't moved it. I knew it was a sign from Lisa and I thought, *If Lisa wants to be here, that's where she'll stay.* The doll has remained in that spot ever since.

– Betty Flores

Sometimes the only healing that grieving parents can find is with the help of the child they have lost. This is especially true in the case of deaths caused by drugs or violence. Some parents of children lost this way end their personal torment when they realize that their children are in a better place. In addition to grief and anger, another overwhelming emotion—guilt—often comes into play for parents whose children have committed suicide. Stories of parents stricken by this emotion are told in the next chapter.

Chapter Six

*Tragic Decisions,
Renewing Encounters*

Sadly, suicide is prevalent problem. The third leading cause of death for children ages fifteen to twenty-four and the sixth leading cause for children ages five to fourteen, suicide leaves family and friends in shock and disbelief. Even if there were signs of depression or unhappiness, often no one suspects their loved one will take that next tragic, irreversible step. When suicide occurs, on top of coping with grief, parents in particular often have to deal with intense feelings of guilt. The questions and "should haves" seem endless.

As the following stories show, sometimes parents do all they can and still lose their children to suicide. Acceptance of their children's choices, along with finding out from after death contacts that their children are finally happy, helps the healing process begin.

Wendy Lynne Sunderlin's arrival into the world on June 18 was dramatic to say the least. I went into labor on a rainy Saturday morning in 1977. On the way to the hospital, the car broke down. An ambulance had to take me the rest of the way. Luckily, Wendy was born healthy.

As Wendy grew from childhood into a wonderful young adult, we all marveled at her attributes. In reality, she may not have been the wisest or the prettiest, but in our world she was both. She graduated from high school in 1995 with a rank of thirteen out of 221 students. That was an awesome feat in my opinion and it enabled her to receive grants and scholarships to attend Ohio Wesleyan University. I was heartbroken that she was going so far away, but I was also very proud of her accomplishments.

Wendy tried hard to fit in and manage the demands of classes, studying and, of course, the new social world into which she was thrust. In December of her freshman year, Wendy attended a party at a fraternity house and, though we never learned all the details, she was apparently the victim of a date rape. That was truly the beginning of the end.

My daughter initially told no one about what happened to her, including me, keeping it locked inside. She came home for Christmas break that month with so much weighing on her mind. After the third week of her vacation, she finally phoned a good friend and unloaded some of the emotional baggage that had built up inside her. When Wendy told her friend about the rape, he didn't know what to say, so he kept quiet and just listened. I guess getting it out wasn't as therapeutic for Wendy as she'd hoped. Instead, she snapped. She took my new husband's prescription medication, went into the bathroom with a knife from our kitchen and cut her wrists. After some time passed with no sounds emanating from within the bathroom, my husband became concerned about Wendy. He decided to check on her to make sure she was alright and thankfully found her before it was too late.

We went to the hospital, where Wendy's wrists were stitched up. Then she was sent to a psychiatric ward for a week. It was at this time that I found out about the rape. I berated myself up for not realizing that something so terrible had happened to my daughter. I had noticed her unhappiness, but never suspected it was due to something as serious and awful as rape. I felt terrible for not being more supportive and understanding during this troubled period in her life.

After the week-long evaluation, the doctors said Wendy was just "overwhelmed" and we had to respect her decisions. She decided to return to school. Though we tried to be supportive, her decision still worried me. I felt she needed to take some time off, but I did as the doctors said and accepted her choices.

She made it through the beginning of the next semester, though she lacked concentration and her grades were suffering. I tried to look on the bright side, remembering that there remained plenty of time to improve and she appeared to be handling her past problems much better. In the spring, she received offers from every sorority on campus to pledge and decided that she wanted to "go for it." She chose Delta Delta Delta and started acting more like her old self. Although I remained concerned, I committed myself to letting her fly on her own like the doctors advised.

Wendy finished the school year, came home for the summer and took two jobs. On the weekends and for a few weekday evenings, she waited tables at a local restaurant and during weekdays, she worked in the factory where her father was employed. She planned to save enough money that summer to go to the Bahamas the following spring to take an extra credit class in marine biology. She would, of course, squeeze in some vacation time there as well.

When she returned to school in the fall of 1996, things were different. She was assigned to live in an older building where the more serious students lived. Her roommates weren't thrilled to be living there, calling it the "boring" dorm. They even went out in the hall and shouted, "Quit studying!" to try to liven the place up.

An amazing thing happened the August afternoon I was there helping Wendy move in. I went outside to get a breath of fresh air. Taking a seat on a bench, I looked up and saw what appeared to be a bunch of stars floating in patterns in the daytime sky. I followed them with my eyes until they started to drift behind some trees. I got up from where I was sitting so I could continue to follow them. One by one they just flew straight up in the sky and disappeared. I was perplexed by this vision. After all, it was a sunny day, not dark at all. I looked around to see if anyone else was there and had seen what I saw, but I was alone. The thought crossed my mind that I might be suffering from heat stroke, but I felt fine. Now I wonder if it wasn't a premonition of some sort. To this day, I'm not sure.

By September, the new school year was in full swing. Wendy was calling home frequently and even phoning me at work just to talk. It was like old times. She met a boy that she really liked and we were so glad that she could commit to someone beyond just a friendship, especially after what she'd been through. I truly thought the worst was behind her. We made plans to go see her for Parents' Weekend in October and she in turn came home the weekend before. It was great fun having her home. We didn't do anything extravagant, just family stuff—a cookout, sitting around our fire pit outside, things like that. On Sunday, we went to the local fair and looked at all the locally grown plants and vegetables. I bought her a cute little pumpkin with flowers painted on it, along with some Indian corn to take back to school with her. On the way home from the fair, she suddenly grew very serious and asked if we were okay financially. We had had to pay for most of her medical bills from the treatment after her suicide attempt out-of-pocket and that bothered her. I assured her that everything was fine.

We went to visit her the following weekend at college for the parent event as planned. She was extremely tired, having gone to a concert in Pittsburgh the night before our arrival. She was upset, because all the scheduled events, including a parade and parties were cancelled due to a tragedy on campus. A fire had broken out in a fraternity house and a young man died in the blaze. We assured her that we understood the reason for the cancellations and that just going to her sorority tea was swell with us. Since she was so tired, we left earlier than scheduled. The curious thing was that in the past whenever we left her at college to go home, she never watched us leave. She always said it made her sad. This time, however, she came out and waved as we drove away.

We spoke on the phone a few times after that and had typical conversations. In early November, during a phone conversation, I noticed she seemed very tense about school and down on herself. I tried to reassure her by saying, "Just do the best you can and you will be fine." I added, "You always have the option of taking a break. The money will be set aside for you to continue one way or the other." I suggested she come home for a weekend before the Thanksgiving break. She sadly said she probably wouldn't be able to since she had so many academic and sorority obligations.

On November 11, 1996, snow started to fall in northeast Ohio. I had to stay home from work that day, because the weather was so bad. Like a kid off from school, I had a grand time, cleaning, cooking, baking and even finishing a stitching project for my upcoming anniversary with my husband.

The next day, even though the snow had not let up, I decided that I should try to make it to my job. It was a slow day at work due to the weather, so I left around 4:00 P.M. I arrived home at 4:30, after a longer commute than normal because of the snow-covered roads. When I opened the garage, I was surprised to see Wendy's car parked there. I was both excited to see her and a bit apprehensive at her sudden and unexpected visit. Why hadn't she called? Why was she suddenly home? Was everything alright?

When I entered the house, everything was quiet. Too quiet. I didn't even take off my jacket. I just removed my wet and snow-covered shoes at the door. My elderly mother was living with us then and was sitting downstairs reading. I asked her about Wendy. She said it was a nice surprise that Wendy had come home and speculated that she was upstairs changing her clothes. I called up the stairs to Wendy repeatedly, but received no answer. I thought maybe she was napping. Curious, I started up the stairs to check on her. At the top of the stairway, I saw something strange splashed all over the inside of the open bedroom door. She must have spilled something, I thought. When I entered her room, I saw a rifle laying next to Wendy. She had shot herself. My beautiful, talented, loving daughter left this world alone and by her own hand.

I fled down the stairs screaming, grabbed the phone and dialed a neighbor. He came running over while his wife called 911. Soon the house was overflowing with paramedics, neighbors, police detectives and sheriffs—with my poor dead daughter upstairs.

I knew my husband would be concerned when he got close to home. We lived on a quiet, rural road that was now swarming with flashing lights and emergency vehicles. I didn't want to be there alone, so I asked the paramedics to stay until my husband arrived.

When he finally came, my husband naturally thought the emergency vehicles were for my mom, because she was eighty-six and not in great health. He was devastated to learn the truth.

Why did Wendy do this? we asked ourselves. We'll never know all the answers. She didn't leave a note. Afterwards, I pieced the information together and determined that she left her dorm at 8:30 that morning as if going to class. Instead, she got in her car and drove home. She never called to say that she was coming. She arrived at our house around 1:00 P.M. At 1:30, she made two calls to the college. We are not sure to whom or why. Then, according to the coroner, she killed herself sometime between 1:30 and 2:00 P.M.

I thought knowing exactly what happened that day would help, but it really didn't. I spent the next year and a half in such deep shock and anguish that I couldn't even do basic household chores. Though I have recovered somewhat, some days I still just wallow around. Other times, when things are bad, I try to be productive, but it takes great effort. I have to make big plans to do something as simple as baking cookies. I read a lot, which helps when I'm feeling down and recently I became a SOLOS guide (Survivors Of a Loved One's Suicide). Through the program, I help others who have been affected by suicide by distributing materials through funeral homes in my area.

In essence, I've coped with my personal tragedy by trying to help others who are in similar circumstances and not just those parents who've lost children to suicide, but those who've lost children for any reason.

In a positive sense, I have become kinder to others and more willing to lend a shoulder to people who are hurting and need to come out of their wounded shell. Before, I was so caught up in my own life that I didn't really notice others and their problems. I do now.

Trivial things mean little to me now. I've learned to prioritize my life better. Of course, this self-improvement has been bittersweet, for life is lackluster without one's only daughter.

Death is one of the hardest things for people to deal with. If my story helps one person, then I guess I've done something worthwhile. Sadly, my Wendy is gone, but she'll never be forgotten. I honestly believe that one day I'll be with her again.

Wendy's Contacts

The very first time I saw or felt Wendy was within forty-eight hours of her death. I could not bring myself to go upstairs for obvious reasons, so I spent all my time in the downstairs living area of our home. I hardly slept, but did try to rest in between bouts of sobbing. All of a sudden, late one night, I saw what looked like a long hallway with a row of doors down the sides. Wendy was standing at the far end. She didn't say anything. She just looked at me with the saddest smile, then turned and walked through the farthest door into a brilliant white light. At first I thought I was hallucinating, but after a new round of tears, I realized that I was wide awake and I had indeed seen Wendy.

The second sighting came about eight weeks later. Her best friend, Owen, became one of our closest friends after the tragedy and spent a great deal of time with us when he wasn't away at college. During his Christmas break he came over one night with a video he rented. He sat across the room from me and my husband on one of the couches. We started the movie. The only lights in the room, aside from the television, were candles. The evening was going along fine. I rested my head back and when I looked up, there was Wendy standing at our front door between the television and the couch where Owen was sitting. Wendy raised her hands up over her head like she was stretching, then smiled at me. I was shocked at the vision. I wasn't dozing nor had I been drinking alcohol. In fact, for the first time in ages, I hadn't even been thinking of her.

I was afraid to say anything at that moment; I didn't want to scare Owen or have him think I was crazy. I did feel better after seeing her and concluded that even though Owen hadn't seen her, she was trying to tell me she was there for him, also.

In December, just over a year after Wendy's death, our neighbors invited us to their house to celebrate the coming New Year. Even though I wasn't feeling up to it, I agreed out of friendship and was determined not to ruin things for the others by being sad. We arrived at the party and I was okay for a while then I began talking about Wendy with my neighbor's daughter-in-law who had come from out of town to spend the holidays. Suddenly, she took my hand as tears came to her eyes. I thought, *Oh boy, I've done it now* and quickly changed the subject. Shortly thereafter, I excused myself from the party and went home. My husband was in a deep conversation with someone, so he stayed behind. I had only been home a few minutes when the phone rang. It was my husband. "Don't go to bed yet. I need to talk to you when I get home," he told me. I wasn't sure why and I was very tired, but I agreed and waited up for him.

When he finally came home, he was very excited. He told me that our neighbor's daughter-in-law—the woman who I'd thought I'd upset with my talk of Wendy—told my husband a fascinating story. The previous year, she and her husband had come to visit for the holidays. One night, after she went to sleep in her in-law's guest room, something woke her up. She opened her eyes and saw a young girl standing in the room. It scared her. She tried to wake her husband, but he was sleeping too deeply. The girl communicated with her telepathically. *Please tell my parents that I'm so sorry for what I did. It was not their fault. I'm so sorry.*

The girl kept repeating how sorry she was for what happened. The vision lasted about a minute. The daughter-in-law didn't know who the girl was, so she kept the story of the appearance to herself. Apparently, when I told her about

Wendy and described my daughter to her at the party, she realized she had seen Wendy in the bedroom that night.

I didn't doubt the veracity of the woman's story for a moment. Wendy had been very close to those neighbors and had spent a lot of time playing in their guest room—the same room where the daughter-in-law saw her. The neighbors used to watch Wendy for me on snow days and after school when she was a young child. It was like a second home to her.

I'm glad I learned of this story and I think it was for the best that it was told to my husband a full year after Wendy's death; we might not have believed it earlier. We were meant to know more about ourselves and Wendy's contacts before this was revealed. The story gave us a great deal of peace. It was another confirmation that Wendy lives on.

For any person traveling a similar journey though life, I wish they find peace on this hard road. It is at best, bumpy, and at worst, the most pot-holed lane one can imagine. Sometimes, it helps to be able to "see" and believe things and not write them off as coincidences or wishful thinking.

– Sharon L. Throop

Sue Upchurch has also traveled the bumpy road that Sharon Throop has been on. And, like Sharon, Sue has found peace and healing through contacts with her daughter.

My Melanie arrived into the world four weeks overdue. She was a happy little girl who didn't know the meaning of the word "stranger." When she joined the Brownies she was always the top salesgirl. She'd walk up to anybody, anywhere, and get them to buy her cookies.

It wasn't until she hit puberty, around the middle school years, that I noticed a sadness in her. I often asked her what was wrong. Her answer was almost always the same: "I don't belong anywhere. I don't have anyone." My two oldest daughters are eighteen months apart and had each other. My younger sons are twelve months apart and thus were very close. My husband and I are a couple. Melanie was right in the middle by herself. That's how she felt. We were a big family of seven and she perceived herself as being all alone.

The chilling part of this is that Melanie was actually a twin. Her sibling died during my pregnancy. When I finally told "Mel" this when she was twelve or thirteen, it was very cathartic for her. "I've always felt inside of me something was missing. This explains it," she said.

Though her sadness seemed temporarily lessened by the news of her lost twin, things soon took a turn for the worse. We began having trouble with Mel when she reached high school. She became rebellious and moody. Sometimes she'd be outspoken and confrontational. Then the next day she'd become quiet and withdrawn. We sent her to counseling, but she ended up play-acting and becoming whatever the therapists wanted her to be so they'd think she was better and end the sessions. In her spare time, she wrote a lot of poems about love and death. Like most parents of teenagers, I figured it was an angst-ridden phase she was going through and she would eventually outgrow it.

Regardless of all the problems, in many ways we remained close. One day, when she was really down, I took her to the mall for some private time. When I asked her what was bothering her, she said, "I'm alright, Mom. It's my problem and I have to handle it. Everything will be okay."

To complicate matters, Melanie fell in with a rough crowd. As she spent more time with them, her moods swings became more volatile and dramatic. She behaved normally for a while, got along with the family and even had fun with us. Then, without warning, she just blew up. During these periods, nothing was ever right in her eyes. She battled us every way she could. The emotional meltdowns usually ended with her running away from home. Each time she did, she stayed away a little longer than the last time. Her attitude and involvement with the wrong kinds of kids got so bad I eventually had to pull her out of school. She later took the GED test and passed it, but even that seemed to set her off. After taking the test, she didn't come home for three weeks. She stayed with other family members and remained in touch, so it wasn't like she just vanished. Still, it was draining to deal with a sixteen-year-old girl who behaved this way. I asked her why she kept doing these things and she simply responded, "I need space." Like so many teenagers, she was deep inside her own world.

When she finally came by for a "visit," we had a nice, calm discussion. I didn't want to scold her, be overbearing or get her upset, so I just let her be. I wanted her to work out the problems she was dealing with and come home when she was ready. Despite her flighty behavior, I knew she wasn't a bad girl. She had a good heart, never tried to hurt anyone, loved animals, enjoyed playing practical jokes on people—especially on me—and was the first to help a friend in need. She often confessed that she didn't know why she did the anti-social things she did. As before, I convinced myself that it was a teenage thing and she would grow out of it.

A week later, I jumped up in bed one night at 1:00 A.M., certain I'd heard a loud noise. I searched the house, but found nothing unusual. I tried to go back to sleep, but remained troubled by the overwhelming feeling that something was wrong. At 2:00 A.M., the doorbell rang. A doorbell ringing that early in the morning rarely means good news—even without the dark premonition that proceeded it. I was too terrified to answer the door and stayed under my covers. It rang a second time. I finally built up the courage to see what was going on. A police officer was standing outside—another bad sign. He said that there had been an accident. I knew instantly that it involved Melanie. "How badly is she?"

"She's alive, right now."

I went to my room to change for the trip to the hospital. When I returned, I noticed that a friend of Melanie's had ridden with the policeman. I motioned for her to come inside and asked her, "Was Melanie driving?" From what the police officer said, I had assumed it was an auto accident. Melanie's friend set me straight. My daughter had shot herself with a small, .25 caliber handgun. My husband told me later I screamed upon hearing the news. I don't remember anything about that instant. All I remember is running to a phone, calling Melanie's father and telling him to meet us at the hospital.

When I arrived, a doctor came into the room where we were waiting and showed us an x-ray. There was a clear path from one side of Mel's skull to the other where the bullet had entered, traveled through and exited.

The doctor said Mel needed immediate surgery to remove blood clots at both the entrance and exit wound areas. Even with that, her chances weren't good. And if she did survive, she would never be the same. I listened, but nothing was sinking in. *On television, miracles happen all the time.* That's the way I was thinking. *Melanie will be okay.*

They let me see her before the surgery. That scared me to death. Her eyes were halfway open, but she wasn't inside. She was gone. I could see it and sense it. The doctors had probably suspected that, too. Even so, they tried their best to save her, performing the intricate surgery and then putting her on full life support. The battle waged to keep her alive was amazing. They had machines everywhere that breathed for her and took over all her bodily functions.

Because of the brain surgery, they had to cut off her waist-length hair. That was another shock. When I saw her afterward, she appeared so small and helpless. I couldn't believe this was my child lying in the bed. Children aren't supposed to die young. They are supposed to survive their parents. Regardless of everything I was seeing—including that dead look in her eyes—I couldn't accept that she wasn't going to make it.

The machines kept Melanie alive for days, even though her condition appeared to be getting worse. I taped photographs of her around the room and displayed her poems and drawings. I wanted the hospital staff to see her as the beautiful, long-haired teenager she was, not the lifeless being that was in the hospital bed now.

The more I visited the hospital and spoke with the nurses and doctors, the more aware of reality I became. Suicide can be done in so many ways—pills, cutting the wrists, gunshots to the body, etc. In all of these instances, the person is crying out for help and still giving herself a chance. However, when a person shoots herself in the head, there's no chance. My daughter had made her decision and she tried to make it permanent. When I finally came to that realization, I decided to take her medical status to "Code O." This meant that the hospital staff still gave her everything she needed to survive—medicine, IV nourishment, respirator—but if anything else happened, they'd let her go. In a way, I felt this was like putting her in God's hands.

Understandably, her father fought me on this. I don't blame him. He was still in the state of denial I'd been in earlier—unable to see the truth and let go. I've always believed that men are usually more realistic and stoic about such things, while women hold out impossible hopes for miracles, so I found our situation grimly ironic.

The doctors did some tests to determine Melanie's true condition. I just happened to be there when they performed these exams. Sometimes I wish I hadn't been, while other times I know I needed to see it. They started out gently, calling her name, pinching her, touching her a bit, moving her. After that, it got rough. They pulled, they pushed hard on her chest, they hurt her to try and get a response. As I watched, my hands were clenched in tight fists and my body was tense. It was a struggle to keep from jumping out of my chair and making them stop. Through it all, no matter what they did, there wasn't a blink out of Melanie, not one twitch. My daughter was almost completely brain dead. The doctors concluded that her condition at that point was the best we could ever hope for.

After those tests, everything was a blur. The next thing I remember, I was in my church, crying. The pastor tried to console me, but how do you console a mother who has been told that her seventeen-year-old daughter is gone? The pastor told me to let her go. It was time. Sad as I was, I knew he was right. I returned to the hospital and told them to let her pass. They advised me to go home, get some sleep, think about it further, then return in the morning.

I did as they asked, but remained resolute in my decision. At the hospital the next day, they slowly began the withdrawal process, turning this off, pulling that out, slowing down the respirator. The doctors explained that the entire process could take a few days.

Although a lot of family members had been around throughout this latest ordeal, at one point, I found myself alone in the room with Melanie. I stroked her face and asked God to not let her suffer. I told God that Mel didn't understand what she had done, that she really needed him now and I was confident that he would love her even more than I had. "It's alright, Mel," I whispered. "Go to God. He's waiting for you. There you will find the love and peace you've been searching for." Just as I finished saying this, the alarms started going off and the nurses ran in. I watched Melanie's heart rate fall from 180 to 160 to 60—and then to nothing. Melanie had done it her way. She had waited until she and I were alone and I told her it was okay to move on.

For the first few days after she passed, I kind of just sleepwalked. People talked to me, but it was like they were just moving their lips without making any sounds. I didn't snap out of it until the day before her funeral. When I rejoined the world, I went to work, choosing Melanie's clothes—her favorite jeans and a shirt with the Disney character "Dopey" on it—buying a wig so she would look like herself, copying her poems to hand out and picking a hat, since she often wore hats.

More than 200 people came to pay their respects. Many of her friends brought their own poems and filled her section of the funeral home with roses. When it came time for the funeral home to close, my youngest son latched on to the coffin, started screaming and wouldn't let go. I had to pry him off. It was very traumatic.

Before she died, I expressed an interest in organ donation to the hospital and had been able to donate her corneas and heart valves. A few days before the following Christmas, I received a card from the organ center informing me that they had used both corneas and both heart valves. Mel had perfect vision and the most beautiful eyes, not to mention the kindest heart. To know that her eyes and heart live on in others means the world to me.

It wasn't until I was writing this account that I realized I don't feel as guilty anymore for having survived her. The pain is still there, however. It has become a part of me. I'm not the same person I was before Mel's death. I cry a lot more easily over both sad and happy occurrences. I don't take things for granted anymore. I'm all too aware of everything going on around me. I knew before how much I loved my children, but it wasn't until I lost Mel that I understood to what extent. They are my heart and soul. There is now a hole in my heart that will be there for the rest of my life. But I'm learning to live with that pain and go on. I still really miss her. There's not a day that goes by that I don't think of her and look at her picture.

Melanie's Contacts

A few months after Melanie's death, my husband decided to take a job offer in Florida. I busied myself preparing to move from our home in North Carolina.

In Florida, I really hit rock bottom. Not only was Melanie gone, but her two older sisters had already made their lives in North Carolina and remained there after we moved. It was almost like I'd lost all three. Plus, suicide is something that most people don't know how to deal with. I lost a lot of the support I had when most of our friends and family distanced themselves and just stopped calling or even talking to us. Still, I felt God brought me to Florida. A professional counselor lives across the street and she has helped me cope with my loss. On top of this, the move hasn't stopped Melanie from coming around. "Mom," I heard someone say one afternoon. "What?" I answered instinctively before realizing that I was alone in the house. At other times, I've felt a slight pressure on my shoulder as if someone has placed their hand there. I'm sure it's Mel letting me know she's okay.

The change of residence has not affected Melanie's propensity to continue to play practical jokes. Our television often clicks off just as a show is reaching its climax. That's Melanie's *modus operandi* all the way.

We returned to North Carolina for the Christmas holidays so the family could be together. I was alternately comforted by being with the family and full of heartache seeing the old places again. I sadly told my husband that I wished I could have just five more minutes with Melanie. He asked what I'd do. I explained that I simply wanted to let her know I loved her and make sure she was alright. On Christmas morning, I dreamed that I was standing in a field with all these people around me, both family members and strangers. Then I realized Melanie was beside me! I became excited and started asking all kinds of questions, but she didn't answer. She just smiled. It was such a beautiful smile, so peaceful and happy. I realized that Melanie was giving me my five minutes—and I wasn't keeping my end of the bargain! I stopped the pestering and just stood beside her, gently touching her and feeling peaceful and happy myself. When I woke up, I felt so good about things. I knew that Melanie had given me the only Christmas present she could—peace for the day.

My daughter, Cindy, has also had powerful dream visits from Melanie. She called me one day bursting with excitement. She said she was standing in a field and Mel came riding up on a horse. Melanie loved horses. In the dream, Mel told Cindy to hop on with her so they could talk. "But you're dead," Cindy protested.

"I know. Get on."

"But you're dead," Cindy repeated.

"It's alright," Mel assured her. Cindy climbed on and off they went. As they rode, Mel told her that she was sorry for the pain she put everyone through. "I didn't realize it would hurt you all so badly. Tell everyone that I'm okay. I'm happy and at peace." They arrived at a building and Cindy got off.

"Are you coming with me?" Cindy asked.

"No. I can't go in there yet. I have more work to do."

Cindy wondered what she meant and turned to study the building. Nothing registered. When she turned back around, Mel was gone. She was never able to solve the mystery of what the building signified and why Mel couldn't go inside. However, when she described the horse Mel was riding, goose bumps rose on my body. It was Mel's favorite horse, an animal Cindy never saw or even knew about.

Melanie visited my oldest daughter, Amanda, as well. In Amanda's dream contact, they were in a room together talking. Amanda was mad at Mel because of what she'd done. "I'm sorry," Mel responded, "but I really want everybody to know that I'm alright." Amanda started crying and said she wanted to be with her sister. "I could show you everything, but you'd probably go crazy because you aren't ready," Mel warned. "You can come with me, but it's your choice." Amanda looked around and found herself in a long corridor with many doors. She was at one end and Mel was at the other. "Pick a door and go through it. That will be the rest of your life," Mel explained. Amanda went slowly down the corridor and touched each doorknob, trying to decide. She finally picked one. When she opened it, her husband and children were there smiling at her. When she looked toward her sister to say goodbye, Mel was gone. Amanda turned back around and walked through the door. She woke up and said, "There is a God." Her husband was sitting up next to her and heard it. He said that he woke up, because she had been crying and talking in her sleep.

These contacts have done the most to help me get through her death. I know she is with God, surrounded by love and at peace. I'm certain I'll see her again one day.

– Sue Upchurch

A child's suicide can cause a parent to question everything in the world—including God. Sharon Staiduhar did just that. Yet it was her son's contacts that renewed her belief in God and gave her hope for the future.

My first husband was an only child and didn't want to have children. He said, "You don't miss what you don't have," but that sure didn't work for me. My heart ached for a child—or two or three! We waited five years because of my husband's reservations, then finally we had one.

My son, Kevin, was just the perfect baby! He was cat-like in the way he could sleep. He'd hit the pillow and snooze for ten to twelve hours a night. Then, during the day, he'd take two three-hour naps. That's eighteen hours a day—just like our cat. When he grew up and started school, I had to break him of that second three-hour nap because there wasn't enough time in the day. Believe me, it wasn't easy!

When he was awake, he was like every other boy, active, playful and full of energy. From early on, his friends began calling him "Ski" because his last name was such a mouthful—Lovenduski. The nickname stuck and became all I, or basically anyone else, ever called him.

Ski grew to be tall and thin. Despite his slender frame, he was quite a good athlete. He excelled at softball, baseball, football, wrestling and bowling.

Every mother loves her children and thinks they're angels, but my Ski was truly beyond the norm in how he showered me with hugs and attention. There was nothing I asked of him that he wouldn't do. Even in his teenage years, he bent over backwards to please me. His father and I divorced when he was young and from that point on he felt a sense of importance, like he was the "man of the house," the protector of his little sister, Robyn, and me.

The years flew by. Ski graduated high school and continued his education at the Electronic Technical Institute. His goal was to transfer to Cleveland State University for his final two years. He was a dedicated student, making the dean's list with a 3.8 average in the tough field of electrical engineering.

Ski was always studying, pouring himself into his chosen field. I was so proud of him.

The week before the start of his senior year, Ski called me into his room. He was very serious. He said that he was feeling strange and was hearing voices in his head. Alarmed, I wanted to make an immediate appointment to see a doctor. "No," he said. "I think it's just a phase all boys go through as they mature. I'll be okay." That was troubling to me because I was sure hearing voices wasn't part of a phase that everyone goes through. I suggested that Ski was working too hard at school and was getting burnt out.

"Maybe you should take the next semester off?" I offered.

"Would that really be okay with you?" he asked, warming to the idea.

"Sure. Take a break."

He stayed home, but things went from bad to worse. He started sitting alone, talking to himself or laughing at some private jokes. When we questioned him about it, he professed to have no knowledge of what we were talking about.

One Saturday morning, he left the house for a dentist appointment and didn't come back. I thought he went directly to his part time job as a cook in a pizza place, but that was unusual because he always called me or came home first. His boss phoned later in the afternoon, wondering where he was. His boss said he saw Ski's car in the parking lot for a while, then it was gone. Days passed and Ski didn't resurface. We checked with his friends and the places he regularly visited, but we couldn't find a trace of him. I called the police, but they said since Ski was an adult, there was nothing they could do. When I pushed them, the officer in charge said, "Ma'am, you might as well face it. Your son is probably laying dead in a ditch somewhere." What a terrible thing to say to a mother! My heart sank and I fell apart. My second husband, George, and I drove around for hours every night searching and searching for him. Finally, on the fifth day, Ski called and meekly asked if he could come home. "Of course you can," I said, too elated to worry about the strangeness of the request. "This is your home." When he arrived, he said that somehow he ended up in Kentucky (from Ohio). He had no memory of driving there, being there or where he stayed for those five days. He just blacked out. That was disturbing, but all I cared about was that he was home and not "laying dead in a ditch."

It took us most of the next day to convince Ski that he needed medical help. He was hospitalized for three days and evaluated extensively. When he was released, I asked what they found. "Don't get upset," Ski told me. "It was just a psychotic episode." *What the heck does that mean?* I wondered. The doctors wouldn't tell me anything since Ski was an adult. They gave him some medication and sent him home.

That night, Ski asked if he could see a friend. "Of course," I said. "You're not a prisoner here." He returned in a half hour saying he was tired. Six hours later, while I was at the restaurant where I worked, I received a call. It was Ski. He was in the emergency room of the local hospital. He had taken a bottle of Advil and every other pill he could find in the house in an attempt to kill himself. He said he had no memory of doing that. All he remembered was waking up, struggling to breathe and feeling pain in his chest. He called 911 and was rescued.

I rushed to the hospital. When I arrived, Ski told me that he was starting to remember things. The voices in his head, he said, ordered him to take all the pills. If he obeyed, they promised to leave him alone.

Co-author Donna Theisen and her son, Michael, the
inspiration for this book. Michael has returned
through butterflies, eagles, stopped clocks, dreams
and computers.

Andy Dawson and his sister, Jill. Andy has appeared to Jill in a dramatic fashion on her college campus.

Deborah Callam and her son Alex. Alex has spoken to his sisters and waved to his mom from a tree branch outside her window.

Justin Harrison and his mother, Libbie. Justin has made contact in a variety of ways, one of which may have saved his mother's life.

Jessica Reed (right), her big sister, Samantha, and her mother, Beverly. Jessica has appeared to her mother and has visited to play her toy piano.

Greg Sangregorio with his dog, King (above), and Greg's sisters and mother, (left to right) Cheri, Gail and Karen. In a dream the night after Greg's death, Gail accurately recreated the violent auto accident and spoke to her son.

Matt Mundt and his mother, Patti. After his death, Matt helped his sister win a raffle prize at the state fair and appeared to his great-grandmother.

Bob Coe and his son, Mike. Mike appears in dreams and through the classical music piece that was played at his funeral.

Keith, son of Linda Zeliger. After his death, Keith has visited his family by playing music from his toy box and causing the car alarm to go off.

Tobin MacDonald before he became ill (left), and with his Grandma Jeanie and brother, Nolan, after losing his hair due to cancer treatments. Tobin has returned in a rustle of angel wings, caused a music box to play and visited his mother.

Christopher Faller with his mother, Maria, and sister, Rachel. Christopher has comforted his mom in a number of visions in which he speaks to her.

Jessica Galbis and her mother, Kathy. Jessica returned in a magical dream where she was inside a globe of light presented to Kathy by a rainstorm of tiny angels.

Dolly and her husband, James (left), and Dolly's mother, Connie Vocale. Dolly stepped out of this Silver Anniversary wedding picture and scolded her mother for mourning her so deeply.

Gerald LeMaster and his mother, Susie. Susie stood guard and diligently chased away the spirits of departed relatives who came to take her sick and dying son, however she was unable to continue the exhausting task indefinitely. After Gerald passed, he appeared to his mother at her bedside.

Michele DeGennaro with her son, Anthony, who sends riddle-like messages in dreams and interrupts his mother's unrelated dreams with strange, out-of-context appearances.

Bryan Forsyth and his mother, Jane. Bryan rings his mom's phones and visits in dreams of butterflies and beautiful fish.

Mike Tiedt (left), his sister, Taya, and his mother, Eileen. Even after his death, Mike continues to teasingly wake his sister by tickling her face with her long hair in the morning—just as he did when he was alive.

Shane Hebert, son of Judi
Walker. Shane sent a rainbow
to his mother and little sisters
and appeared to his mother
as she drove down the street.

Monika Hedglin with her son,
Joshua, who has communicated with
her through a talking teddy bear.

Brian Hotchkiss and his mother, Phyllis.
Phyllis dreamt of angels taking Brian
away on the night of his murder—before
she knew anything about it. Brian has
since returned in dreams and launches
books from a shelf.

Lisa, daughter of Betty Flores. Lisa has
called out to her mom from behind the
front door and moved a look-a-like
porcelain angel doll.

Photo by Olan Mills

Wendy Sunderlin (left), and with her mother, Sharon. Wendy has materialized in various areas near her home, including a room in a neighbor's house where she used to play as a child.

Melanie Brown in her kitchen and with her family at her sister's wedding. Melanie's teasing and playful attitude comes through in her contacts like turning off the television during a program's climax.

Original photo by Raimor Studios.
Restoration by the Rich Pappas Studio

Kevin "Ski" Lovenduski (above), and his mother, Sharon, Sharon's husband, George, and Ski's sister, Robyn. Ski walked over and around his mother in her bed at night with the soft paws of a cat.

Shari, daughter of Donna Stroyan. A chorus of unseen "angel" birds serenaded Donna on the morning of Shari's funeral. Shari's spirit has thrown things when uneasy and has appeared as a chattering little girl.

Chris, as a child, and his mother, Ricki Zaracki, with her husband, Ray. Both Chris and Ricki had dreams that foretold his murder. After his death at the age of seventeen, Chris sent comforting messages to his heartbroken and grieving mother.

Devoted schoolteacher Gaye Parnell and her family. Sensing her foster baby, Billy, would soon be taken away and reunited with his troubled relatives, Gaye spent time one night holding him. Hours later, Billy was taken away—he died of SIDS.

Kevin Thomas Bowles, his mother, Martha, and Martha's husband, Jim. For years, Martha dreamed that her son would die when he was twenty. He did and miles away, Martha sensed the exact moment when it happened. Kevin subsequently conversed with his mother in dreams and appeared to her right before she underwent surgery.

Mike Howe and his mother, "Motivated On-Line Moms" founder, Bonnie Blankenship. Both Mike and Bonnie had strong premonitions that a vacation in Central America would be Mike's undoing. It was. Three months after his death, he appeared to Bonnie in her kitchen and bid her a proper farewell.

Brad Moore (far right), with his sisters, Laurie and Heather, his mother, Linda, and his father, Jim. In an awe-inspiring dream, Linda followed Brad into "the land of Oz" and later received a "heavenly caress."

Keith David Stenrose with his parents and younger brother (left), and with his wife, Beth, and their baby daughter, Brittany. Keith visited his mom, Rose, at her bedside and sends messages to his sister through books and shooting stars.

Sheri Tabler and her son, Jeremy. Jeremy made miraculous contact with his mother through a photograph on the day of his death.

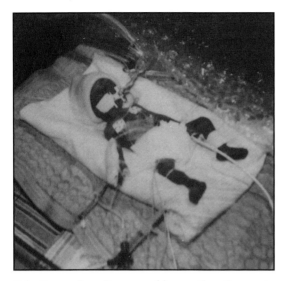

Baby Joanna Jean Bruner and her mother, Susan. A young girl bathed in a warm light hovered over Susan's bed. Was it Joanna Jean?

Amanda Harris and her mother, Sue. Amanda's spirit makes toy rattles play their music— something she was never strong enough to do in life.

Betsy Watson and her son Luke. Luke let his mother know he'd continue to be the light of her life even after his death.

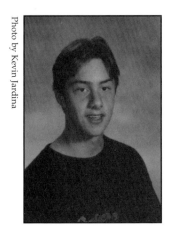

Dylon Velard (left), and with his siblings and mother, Barbara, hunting for the perfect Christmas tree. Dylon's little sister witnessed Dylon's passing and later, when Barbara underwent surgery, Dylon showed up at her hospital bedside to watch over her.

Casey Russell (left), and his family: parents Frank and Beth and siblings Corey and Kerri. A dewdrop kiss and a train whistle in answer to his mother's question are the gifts given by Casey at Bat.

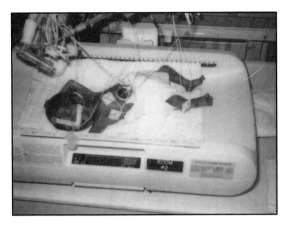

Jack Hooyer (above) and his mother, Amy. A tiny hug and a spoken word of love are the blessings left by Jack.

Lynn Rosecrans with her son, Nicholas Owen. Nicholas has visited Lynn's friend in dreams.

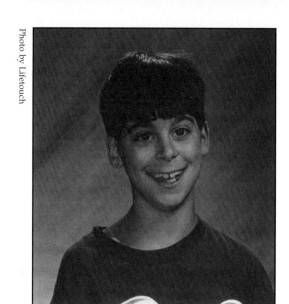

Justin Daniels (above), and with his family (clockwise): sisters Kristle, Sierra and Kelsey, mother Tamera and father Patrick. Justin's contacts have been so numerous and frequent Tamera chronicled them in a diary.

Ski remained in the hospital for two weeks. He was diagnosed as a paranoid schizophrenic and was given additional medications. During this latest evaluation, the counselors told me something odd. They said that Ski and I were "very meshed" and indicated that this was something negative. I asked them to explain and they said, "You are very close to each other. You depend upon him and he depends upon you. That's not good for a child." I thought how awful that a professional counselor could feel this way. It was the greatest thing in the world to be close to your family, especially your children. They were taking something I felt was wonderful about my life with Ski and turning it into some maternal guilt trip, the "co-dependency" stuff that was the pop psychology flavor of the month at that time. It really upset me.

Ski was also upset—emotionally and physically. He hated the medication he was supposed to take because it made him sick to his stomach, lethargic, stiffened his body and stripped him of his ambition. Because of this, he eventually stopped taking the medicine. He decided that he'd rather deal with the illness itself, which was growing progressively worse, than suffer through all the side effects of the medication. I begged him everyday to try again, assuring him that the troubling reactions would wear off. He wouldn't listen.

I came home from work one day and found all the lights in the house on, the water running full blast in every sink, the washer, dryer and dishwasher spinning with nothing inside, and the outdoor sprinklers engaged. "Ski, what's going on? Did you do this?" I asked.

"Do what, Mom?" he answered. "Why are you blaming me?"

He repeated this "house in an uproar" activity a number of times and in each instance, he proclaimed innocence. At the same time, he began to develop a hot temper that was like nothing I'd ever seen before. I became very afraid of what was going on inside him, so scared that I could hardly sleep at night. Something terrible was happening to my precious son and nobody seemed to be able to help him.

I went back to the mental health agency over and over until I got tired of hearing their rote reply—"If he's not a threat to himself or anyone else, there is nothing we can do."

"He tried to commit suicide!" I reminded them. "I think he's clearly a threat to himself!"

Still, no one would help. I felt like I was in this fight all alone, so I became determined to battle for him. I read all I could about paranoid schizophrenia, joined support groups and did everything else I could possibly think of. I learned that schizophrenia is a predisposition that you are born with. There's no way to prevent it from coming and no way to anticipate the episodes. Many people think it's related to drinking and drugs, but that's not true. Ski didn't drink or do drugs and he suffered from this mental illness terribly, as bad as one can imagine. If treated with the proper medications and with the proper attention from doctors, paranoid schizophrenics can lead normal lives. They can work, get married and even find contentment. I found all this knowledge encouraging.

Ski returned to school in March, but was not the student he had been before. He missed classes and didn't study very much. In late September, he vanished again. For a whole month, there wasn't any sign of him. A friend of his told us that he was living in his car deep in the woods somewhere, because the voices told him not to come home. Finally, after the weather turned bitterly cold, he resurfaced. He phoned a number of friends asking if he could stay with them, but they refused because of his strange behavior. With no other option, he called me. He explained that the voices convinced him that "we"—his family—were out to get him and he had to stay away from us. It took us a long time to persuade him that it wasn't true.

My son became painfully lonely during this period. He wanted his friends back and wanted things to be the way they were before he became so ill. Part of the problem was his sickness, of course, but another part was that his friends were simply growing up and moving on. They were going to college, getting jobs, uprooting to other towns, getting married—basically becoming adults. Ski, on the other hand, because of his illness and draining medications, appeared to be frozen in time. My heart ached for him.

After months of studying his condition and going from one mental health agency to another, I finally found a human being who really cared. I met a healthcare case manager who turned out to be an angel. She visited Ski, arranged to have him receive his medication treatments by injection so he wouldn't have to take the pills, drove him to the doctor's office for regular appointments and frequently called to check on him. She really became a friend. She also enrolled him in support groups and directed him to a "big brother" type who took him fishing and bowling. For a while, everything was going nicely. I was convinced that Ski was going to pull out of the darkness and be okay.

Then one day, Ski called me at work. He was frantic. "Please come and get me!" he begged. "The people are making me throw all my clothes away and I'm scared." I immediately picked him up from work and took him back to the hospital. He stayed another five days and was released as before. After that, the voices in his head apparently became stronger and more demanding. *Throw all your furniture away and we will leave you alone. Throw all you're your books away and we will leave you alone. Throw all your money away and we will leave you alone*, they told him. He was so desperate to quiet the voices that he kept doing as he was told, which included tossing $3,000 in cash into a river.

Not only were the voices tormenting Ski, they deceived

him as well and Ski knew it. He would say to me, "Mom, why do they lie to me? I do everything they ask and they still come back and keep telling me what to do next. They try to scare me." Ski was in such agony over this and I was powerless to help him.

One evening, he told me that he was too afraid to sleep, that something bad might happen if he did. I suggested that he take a hot bath to relax, then watch some television and he'd be okay. "Oh no, Mom!" he exclaimed. "I can't do that. What if the TV catches on fire and I die?" He was so afraid, paranoid and obsessed with staying alive. No matter how bad things became, he didn't want to die.

We called the doctors nearly a half dozen times begging to have Ski hospitalized again, but they didn't feel it was warranted. I was told to double up on his medication and he would be fine.

On Mother's Day in 1995, Robyn came home from college, picked up Ski and brought him to the restaurant where we were going to have dinner to celebrate the holiday. My children presented me with a dozen long stemmed red roses. It was the nicest Mother's Day I've ever had. The following morning, Ski said he had an earache and wanted to see a physician. As we sat in the waiting room, I noticed him staring at me intently. "Why are you looking at me like that?" I asked.

"Because you're so pretty, Mom. And you're the only person in the world I can trust. You've been the best mother anyone could ever want. You've been so good to me and Robyn. When I get better, I'm going to finish college, get a good job and take care of you so you won't have to work so hard."

The next morning, while I was at work, a nurse came to my home to give Ski his shot. She found him sitting in a chair with a plastic bag over his head. My precious son, tormented with pain and frustration, had suffocated himself.

The mental health personnel speculated that Ski must have heard voices so forceful and powerful that he became frozen with fear. As before, the voices must have ordered him to kill himself and then they would leave him alone. He didn't leave a note, which wasn't surprising, because I knew how much he wanted to get better and beat the illness. He obviously wasn't acting out of his own free will.

My life basically ended that day. I have a hole in my heart that will never be repaired. I cry every day for Ski and miss him terribly. I'll never be the same again. I've prayed that in time I'll heal to some extent. I have a beautiful daughter, Robyn, and a wonderful husband, George, and I need to hold on for them. They shouldn't have to see me sad, depressed and crying every day. However, until someone walks in the shoes of a parent who has lost a child, they will never understand the real pain we suffer. Life just loses its meaning. Things that interested you before are of no consequence. You feel so alone and scared. I pray to God to help me through this, but it's such a long, slow process.

Ski's Contacts

When people lose their parents, they usually cling closer to their faith in God, taking comfort that their elderly mother or father is happy, healthy and in a better place. That's not necessarily the case when you lose a child. Parents who lose a child often find their faith in God is shattered. It's such a shocking, unbearable pain you can't imagine a loving God doing that to you. Like so many others, I struggled with my once unshakeable faith. I always believed that I'd see my parents again. With Ski, there was doubt. Instead of assurance, I was terrified that I'd never see him again. My faith just dissolved.

At Ski's funeral, I prayed passionately to God that he would give me a sign that Ski was really in Heaven, that he could still hear me when I spoke to him. That night when I went to sleep, I again fervently prayed: "Please, Ski, let me know you can hear me. Please give me a sign, anything so I know you're safe."

As I drifted to sleep, I noticed that our cat, Tinsel, was especially animated. She was walking all over the bed. I could feel her paws by my feet, chest and by my head. I could even feel her breath on my face. As Ski's condition had worsened, my husband often told me Tinsel was the closest thing to Ski, even closer than me. My boy who slept like a cat when he was a baby had bonded with this cat as he neared the end. Because of this, I figured that Tinsel sensed something had happened to Ski and was out of sorts that evening. I just ignored her and went to sleep. Throughout the night, I woke up briefly to feel Tinsel's paws still rambling all over the place.

"Tinsel was such a little pest last night," I told George the next morning. "She kept walking all over me. She came up by my head, then down by my feet and back and forth all night long. I could hardly sleep."

George got ready for work, gave me a kiss and left. The next thing I knew, he was back in my bedroom. His face was ashen. "How could Tinsel have been walking on the bed?" he stammered. "She was outside all night! I just let her in."

We both knew instantly that it wasn't Tinsel—it had to have been Ski. God was answering my prayers and giving me the sign I'd asked for that told me Ski was okay.

Later that day, needing to believe that it was really Ski, I prayed for just one more sign, a confirmation of sorts. That night, I again felt the little paws all along the bed and even from under the bed. It felt like someone or something was pushing up on the mattress, ever so lightly. Once again, this had to have been Ski. God answered my prayer again and I knew my son was alright.

– Sharon Staiduhar

Whether dramatic or subtle, after death contacts not only help parents say goodbye to their children, they help them find solace after experiencing the trauma of their children taking their own lives. As the next story tells, the contacts helped Donna Stroyan remember that life can still have joy and laughter even after the loss of her daughter.

I was working at the YWCA late one afternoon and was suddenly overwhelmed by a sense of dread. The sky was growing dark, threatening a nasty summer storm. I had numerous reasons to feel anxiety about the weather. My husband was on the road returning from Boston six hours away. My youngest daughter was outside playing lacrosse for her high school's junior varsity team. And my oldest daughter, Shari, had gone downtown with friends to rent tuxedos for the upcoming high school prom. My thoughts centered upon my youngest daughter. She appeared to be the most vulnerable to the lightning that was sure to precede the thunderstorm. I dashed to a phone to see if Shari was home. I wanted her to drive over to the school to check up on her sister.

There was no answer. I began to feel more anxious. A distinct voice sounded inside my head. *Go home*, it said. I glanced at my assistant. She was reading a story to a large group of children we supervised as part of an after school program. I knew there were simply too many kids for her to handle alone. Plus, I didn't feel I could justify leaving by saying I heard a voice in my head. *Go home*, the voice repeated. I looked outside. It was darker and the rain was pounding. *It's just the storm making you nervous*, I told myself. I finished work an hour later and headed for my house.

I was surprised to see my husband arrive from his long trip at exactly the same time I got home from work. When I also saw Shari's car and realized she had returned home as well, I breathed a deep sigh of relief. Taking some things I'd recently purchased for Shari's upcoming birthday out of my trunk, I headed toward the front door of the house.

The moment I entered the house, I felt something was wrong. It was eerily dark inside. Why hadn't Shari turned on the lights? Yet I momentarily ignored my fears, preoccupied as I was with quickly hiding the gifts I'd bought for Shari. The next day she'd be turning seventeen. She was blossoming into a beautiful young woman and I wanted to make this birthday extra special. After stashing the gifts in a back closet, the concern and worry I had initially felt returned, so I decided to go upstairs to check on my daughter.

As I reached the top of the stairway, I was transfixed by the most amazing sight. Shari was leaning high against the wall by the doorway that led into her room. A soft light from an adjacent window was shining on her upturned face. Her lips were parted as if she was speaking. Her palms were turned forward. Her strange posture struck me as being in supplication to the Lord. For a few seconds, I was both entranced and mystified by the powerful sight. Then I noticed that her feet were not touching the floor. A wave of horror immediately obliterated the strange tranquility I had been feeling. I screamed in agony. My daughter, my beautiful teenage daughter, had hung herself with a belt.

At the sound of my screams, my husband rushed upstairs to find me trying to get Shari down. He immediately sprang into action to help me. Though I knew she was dead, when we got her down I still made a desperate attempt to breathe life into her body while my husband ran to call 911. After a few moments, I stopped and just talked to Shari, telling her I loved her, explaining that I could have forgiven her for whatever she did that made her take her own life.

Suddenly, my thoughts turned to my younger daughter. I sensed she was okay, that I didn't have to worry about her, but I didn't want her to see what happened to Shari. I went to the phone to call a friend. I asked my friend to pick up my daughter and keep her until we came by later.

Soon the police and paramedics were swarming all over the house. Shortly after they arrived, I felt a searing pain in my stomach. I could no longer function. I was taken to the hospital in the ambulance, and another was called for Shari. My pain must have been psychological, because there was nothing the emergency room doctors could do to ease it.

I couldn't stop crying for days. I even cried in my sleep. It was so odd to wake up crying. I hated being confronted each morning with the realization that the nightmare was actually real.

Flashbacks assaulted me. Anything remotely connected with Shari—a familiar song on the radio, a specific word or phrase she used to use, dark skies, storms, Wednesdays, belts—brought it all back. Even the ghoulish images that surround Halloween brought back haunting memories of the vision of her hanging outside her room.

Shari left behind a series of long letters that explained in detail all the frustrations in her young life that had tortured her so. They were typical things involving school, her social life and a sense of not being understood. It was both sad and illuminating. I realized I had no clue what had been going on in her mind.

I've since committed myself to helping others. Whenever I feel sad, I try to think of someone else who needs care. I wish that suicides would cease, that no other mother would have to suffer what I did. This, of course, has not come to pass, nor will it. I reach out in sorrow and support to those who have lost loved ones to suicide. Day by day, life can become bearable, even joyful and beautiful. Hope is timeless. It lives in the present and future. Look for hope among the living.

Shari's Contacts

On the day of Shari's funeral, I was awakened to the most glorious sound. I listened for a while as the haze of sleep lifted and realized that the large maple tree outside was filled with a flock of birds. I'd never heard anything like it before. It put my soul at ease. I enjoyed their heavenly singing for ten minutes or so, then got up to see what they looked like so I could try to identify the species. To my surprise, the tree was empty! Either they all instantly flew away or they were never there to begin with. Maybe they were a chorus of angels sent to comfort and serenade me on that horrible day, to tell me that life goes on and things wouldn't always be as awful as I imagined.

Three days later, my daughter and I went to the cemetery to salvage some of the lovely baskets and floral arrangements placed on Shari's grave. When we arrived, I was shocked to find them knocked over and scattered about. Before I could get upset at the thought of someone doing such a careless thing, my daughter pointed down the hill. Two small rabbits were sitting nose to nose in the fresh grass. One shot straight up in the air. When it hit the ground, they began chasing each other in circles. The larger rabbit leaped into the air again. My daughter and I couldn't help but laugh. It was so odd, and nice, to be able to laugh again—especially at Shari's grave.

When I returned home, the first thing I noticed was an Easter basket Shari had left in the dining room. I looked inside and was startled to see that the only items there were two miniature chocolate rabbits sitting nose to nose. I gently took them out and placed them on a shelf. It's been nearly a decade and those rabbits remain there to this day.

Although some contacts have been pleasant, others have been quite the opposite. One night, I dreamed I was in the dining room of my childhood home. Shari was standing nearby in the dark. I reached out to her. She grew angry and began grabbing things off the shelves and throwing them at me. I woke up in both physical and emotional pain and was wracked with tormenting guilt. *Had I failed her as a mother? Should I have sensed her secret unhappiness and done something to change her fate? Why didn't I go home when I heard the voice inside my head? If I had, would I have been able to save her? Why hadn't I listened?* I rubbed my arms and chest. I felt sore in the spots where Shari had hit me with the objects she threw.

A few nights later, I had a vivid dream that I was Shari. I felt all her terrible pain and hopelessness. I found myself, as Shari, going through the motions of preparing to hang myself. Fortunately, I woke up before actually reliving the death, but that did little to ease my anguish. I began suffering from one illness after another. My doctor soon put me on antidepressants. She felt my sinking emotional health was affecting my physical well-being.

The antidepressants helped some, but they didn't stop the life-like dreams and visions. The next one came when I was certain I was awake. Shari walked through the front door and announced "I'm only visiting." I was so happy that I again tried to hug her, which was something she always hated. She backed away, which wasn't unusual. I followed her toward the bathroom and she backed all the way to the bathtub. Cornered, she shoved me hard. Naturally, that brought with it new waves of guilt.

Thankfully, as time passed, the contact dreams became more uplifting. One morning as I was lying in bed, I heard the spirited voice of a little girl. I was sure it was Shari speaking. And it struck me as perfectly normal to hear this little girl talk on and on because Shari had been a chatterbox. With great drama and flourish, she told me about her day.

What she had done was nothing special, just routine things, but to her it was clearly important. I listened for a few more moments then opened my eyes to look at her, but she was gone. This time, there was no guilt, just sadness for my loss.

Two years later, on a visit to Shari's grave for her birthday, I was comforted by the sight of two large rabbits sitting on each side of her gravestone as if posing for a photograph. I knew then that God was using the rabbits to remind me of the joy and wonder of life still available to me if I'd allow them to return. More importantly, God was telling me that Shari was no longer sad and angry and had forgiven me.

– Donna Stroyan

It is easy for those who have not experienced them to dismiss after death contacts as wishful thinking on the part of bereaved parents. However, as the previous stories relate, some of these experiences are unexpected, unwelcome and even frightening, while others are searched for and bring comfort. Some bring guilt and turmoil, while others bring solace and peace. Though intangible and unexplainable, these contacts are vividly real to those open and accepting enough to receive them. Most important, these contacts give the often guilt-ridden parents of children who commit suicide the opportunity to forgive their children and themselves.

Sometimes, through contacts, supernatural occurrences not only happen after the child dies, but before the death even takes place. In the next chapter, parents and children experience ominous dreams and other portents of fate, yet the parents are still able to find some consolation in their children's after death contacts.

Chapter Seven

Frightening Premonitions, Unbreakable Bonds

Most people have felt at one time or another an overwhelming sense of dread or concern about the future. Some people, however, have had moments in which future events are so clear and unmistakable in their minds that such thoughts or images are nothing short of premonitions. Sadly, the premonitions in the following stories are frightening visions of tragedies. Yet perhaps it is the kind of people who have premonitions that are most receptive to receiving healing messages from the children they have lost.

My first son was a picky eater. I repeatedly took him to the doctor to see why he wouldn't eat for days at time. The doctor always assured me that he was fine and would eat when he was hungry. When my second son, Christopher, was born, I reminded myself not to become paranoid over his eating habits. Well, he weighed nine pounds at birth and eating was never a problem. At five months, he was gulping down seventy-two jars of baby food a week and from there, his appetite never stopped. When I think of him, my memories are always filled with visions of him eating. By his mid-teens, he was a strapping six feet tall and weighed 215 pounds.

In contrast to his burly size, Chris was a sensitive child. He adored animals and brought home more strays than I could count. He loved to fish, play football and socialize with his friends.

When Chris was seven, he wrote me a disturbing note that I never forgot. He scribbled down that he felt he was going to die young and added that it scared him. He was distraught over this for weeks. I ended up taking him to our minister so Chris could be assured that he had nothing to worry about.

I had divorced Chris's father by then and I think that may have been bothering Chris as well. I bought him a big teddy bear, sprayed my perfume on it and told him to take the bear with him whenever he visited his dad. I told him if he became frightened about anything, he should hug the bear and know I was with him. As the years went by, Chris carried that bear with him every time he left home. We dubbed it "The Traveling Bear." When I had to be hospitalized for a hysterectomy, Chris sprayed his cologne on "The Traveling Bear" and let me borrow it for a while.

Seeking to form a tighter bond with God, I converted to the Mormon church when Chris was fourteen. I was surprised when he decided to join me. I found out then that Chris had been secretly studying the Bible for years and had a close, deeply personal relationship with God, of which I had been unaware. He hadn't said anything because at that age, I guess, worshiping God isn't "cool."

Shortly after our conversions, Chris and I both started having dreams about Chris dying. I never told him about mine, because I didn't want to frighten him. His own dreams were bad enough. I did tell some of the sisters at the church and they suggested that perhaps God was warning us or preparing us. I couldn't accept that. I tried hard to put their words out of my mind.

On Mother's Day, 1995, Chris gave me a thank you card instead of a Mother's Day card, saying it was more appropriate. He also gave me a tape with a song on it titled "I Miss You." I cried when I played the tape and asked Chris why he gave it to me. "You'll understand," he responded.

A few weeks later, I woke up in the middle of the night and discovered Chris sitting alone in the family room. I asked him why he wasn't in bed. "I had the worst dream as soon as I fell asleep, Mom. It was so real this time. I remember dying." As he said those words, I felt my blood run cold in my body. I was too afraid to ask him what happened in the dream for fear that it would come true, but he told me anyway. He said he had just gotten off work at the pizza parlor and went to visit his best friend. A group of their buddies were hanging out across the street in a vacant lot. Chris was walking over to join them when an unfamiliar car drove up. Someone inside the car pulled out a shotgun and started firing. Chris said he was hit in the head, fell backward to the sidewalk and died. Alarmed, I told him that a dream that powerful might be a premonition. I begged him to stay away from his best friend's house. "I'm going to get killed anyway," Chris responded. "I know I am. I've always known it. So what good is it to just stay home all the time?" Hard as I tried, I couldn't convince him to change his mind.

Chris worked the late shift at the pizza place and usually didn't get off until two or three in the morning. On July 17, 1995—twelve days after his seventeenth birthday—he changed his routine and left work shortly after midnight. It had been a long, hectic night of delivering pizzas and he wanted to wind down with his friends. Despite my request, he went over to his best friend's house just as he did in his dream.

At 12:20 A.M., my phone rang. A youth on the other end told me to come quickly to Chris's friend's street. "Chris just got shot!" the boy told me. I looked at the clock. I knew it was way too early for Chris to be off work, so I suspected this was some kind of sick practical joke. I tried to get information to see if it was true.

"Who is this?" I demanded. "Is Chris hurt?"

"Yeah, he's hurt. His brains are all over the street!"

Remembering Chris's dream, thoughts of the call being a joke vanished from my mind. I jumped into my truck barefoot and raced to the street where Chris's friend lived. Before I arrived, I could see the flashing lights of dozens of police cars in the distance. My body tensed. As I approached, I noticed there was no ambulance on the scene, so I figured they had already taken Chris to the hospital. Frantic, I practically drove over the yellow police tape before coming to a halt. I jumped out and confronted the first officer I saw. "Where is my son?"

"Who are you?" he questioned. I told him about the call and asked where Chris had been taken. The next thing I knew, a half dozen police officers surrounded me. They started grabbing at me and pulling me away. I heard a blur of voices, but only one stood out. "Your son is dead."

As those horrible words hit me, I spotted something out of the corner of my eye. There was a body lying across the sidewalk covered by a sheet. I screamed and tried to get to the body, but the police held me back. I was so determined, they had to handcuff me to keep me from breaking away. "Half his head is gone," an officer screamed in my face. "You don't want to see him like that. There's nothing you can do."

I felt like my soul went straight to hell at that moment. I screamed in agony, lost control of my bladder and fought with all my might to get to my boy so I could just hold him.

The police kept me handcuffed and restrained for more than an hour. I watched in shock as they walked around my son's body, stepped over it and took pictures. There were neighbors all around gawking at him and me. The only way I could escape the nightmare and leave the scene was by convincing myself that it was all a terrible dream, that God wouldn't do this to me and I would wake up and everything would be back to normal. Years have passed and I'm still trying to wake up.

The boys who killed my son were apprehended that same morning. There were four of them in the car and they had been driving around town all night, smoking pot and looking for trouble. There was no motive for the shooting. They just wanted the sick thrill of killing someone. The police had pulled them over thirty minutes earlier for a broken tail light. The officers didn't smell the marijuana and had no legal reason to search the vehicle. If they had, they might have found the sawed off shotgun hidden under the seat loaded with deadly slugs.

As the details emerged, I was stunned to realize that the shooting happened exactly as it did in Chris's dream. Same place, same time, same method: drive-by shooting to the head with a shotgun as he was crossing the street.

I was in total shock for the first four or five months after Chris's death. I moved out of my home and rented an apartment—with little memory of doing so. After the shock wore off, the pain was unbearable. To numb my pain, I started drinking. I stayed drunk for the better part of the next nine months. I even tried to kill myself one night with an overdose of an antidepressant, but I only slept for a couple of days. There are no words to describe the anguish I was experiencing.

When a child is murdered, there is the added misery of having to endure the seemingly never ending court proceedings. I was in no shape mentally or physically to attend the trials, so I sent relatives to sit in for me. The shooter was sentenced to life in prison, the driver received twenty-five years to life, one of the boys in the back seat got two years for "accessory to murder" and the fourth was let go in exchange for testifying against the others.

I've learned many things since I lost my son. People act as if they're terrified of mothers whose children have been murdered. I think they fear it's contagious. Many of the people I was once close to abandoned me after my son's murder. The few who didn't had no idea how to behave around me so they ended up pretending that my son's death never happened. No one talked about Chris or called on his birthday, death day or on any holidays. I felt alienated and ostracized. I still do. Those friends and relatives that left me to deal with this tragedy alone I've simply cut out of my life. I've decided to focus on the few people who have been supportive, especially my son, my daughter and my grandchildren. That's enough for me.

I've also had difficulty dealing with people who think they have all the answers about grieving. Though I know they mean well, I hate hearing, "You'll get over it in time." I had a child for seventeen years. I can't just "get over" losing seventeen years of love. I've had well-meaning people say, "You're so strong. I know you can handle this." But sometimes I feel I can't. People think I'm strong, because I've put up a good, hard front to those in my circle. Inside, however, I'm shattered.

The only light in my tunnel is that after several months of being so angry with God for letting this happen, I've finally come back to Him. I remember sitting crumpled on the floor in my apartment crying out to God, "I'm too angry to talk to you. If you want me, you'll have to hold on to me. I just can't hold on to you." He listened and held on, sending reassurances and comfort. I will never have total peace on earth, but I know when it's my time to leave here, I will be with my son. We'll be together with our Heavenly Father. That's what I cling to now. I pray every night that God will embrace Chris with all the love in heaven until I can be there with my son.

The Traveling Bear that comforted Chris all those years went on one final journey with him. I placed it inside Chris's casket.

Chris's Contacts

Despite the premonitions we both had, my contacts with Chris have not been very dramatic. The most memorable one occurred after my friend told me her dog, a big Labrador retriever mix named Cajun, was going to be put to sleep because of age and irreversible illnesses. Knowing how he loved animals, I thought it appropriate to ask Chris to be there when Cajun passed over, to take care of her and to let me know in some way that Chris had the dog with him. I also prayed to God for permission to allow this to happen. A few days later, I was in the car and absentmindedly turning the radio dial when I stopped on a station playing Chris's favorite song. At that very moment, I had an overwhelming sense that Chris and Cajun were together. I arrived home a short time later and heard from my friend. Cajun had been put down at the exact same time the song played in my car.

Before he was killed, Chris and I made an agreement

that when I eventually died, I would come back and let him know I was all right. Though he wanted to know I would be okay in the after-life, the thought of a sudden appearance by his dead mother was too creepy for my son. He told me, "Don't show up where I can see you! That would scare the hell out of me!" I agreed to call him on the phone instead. If, for whatever reason, I wasn't able to speak, I promised to make the phone ring differently so he would know it was me. Well, a month after Chris passed, the phone began making this strange "dink, dink, dink" sound around midnight once or twice a week. When I moved out of my house and into the apartment, I figured that the sounds would end, but they continued there. I've moved two more times since then, changing telephone equipment, and at every location the new telephones continued to "dink" late at night. Sometimes, when I was really missing him and feeling down in the dumps, I asked Chris to ring the phone for me and he did. As the years passed, it happened less and less frequently until it finally stopped.

– Ricki Zaracki

Sometimes premonitions are not visions of exact future events. Instead, as Gaye Parnell relates, they can be vague and unclear. She knew her foster child would be leaving her, but she never suspected it would be in death.

We had a foster child, Billy, who came to us when he was three months old. Billy had been severely abused. His ribs were cracked numerous times. He had already endured incredible pain at such a tender age. We were his second foster parents in his short life, because the first set couldn't handle him. He wasn't a bad baby. It was just that he cried constantly. The doctors said that was probably why he was abused to begin with. Either something was hurting him that couldn't be diagnosed or he was simply a crier. It was so bad that even when he was drinking from a bottle, he would take a breath, cry, suck on the bottle, take a breath, cry, suck on the bottle. It was maddening!

I'm a tolerant sort, especially when it comes to children, but this baby was driving my whole family crazy. I mean, it was constant crying, day and night. My husband, Bill, and I had recently adopted another baby who was just four months old and Billy's crying was really upsetting her. We had a teenager and a pre-teen of our own as well and they were about ready to pull out their hair.

Although I knew my whole family was suffering, I just couldn't bear giving up on poor Billy, as his parents and his first foster parents had. I didn't want him to have a new set of parents every month. That would be too traumatizing.

One night, at 4:00 A.M.—to the background din of Billy's wails—I prayed with a passion that was beyond anything I'd felt before. I begged God to help me out with Billy, because I knew we were reaching the ends of our ropes. I had held off making this request for weeks since I tend to be independent and didn't want God to think I was a nag. I try to solve problems on my own to the best of my ability. But nothing was working with Billy, so I had no choice but to ask for some divine intervention.

Well, the next morning, Billy stopped crying! Within days, he was cooing, laughing and acting like a regular baby. What a relief! And what a joy for everyone!

As we were celebrating Billy's good fortune, an HRS (Health and Rehabilitation Services) representative called and informed us that they were planning to place Billy with his paternal grandmother. They would come and get him as soon as they completed their standard investigation of her. That troubled me because the lady's son was the person who had allegedly abused the child. This man was scheduled to be released from the military and would no doubt return home to live with his mother. That would place the possible abuser and the abused child under the same roof again. Unfortunately, as a foster parent, it wasn't my place to comment on or have input into such matters. I had to bear with it and hope for the best.

The next few weeks were wonderful. Billy's crying fits didn't return and I was really starting to bond with the baby. However, in the back of my mind, I knew that any second the phone could ring and I'd have to give him up. Although I've cared for many foster children, it always hurts to lose a child, especially if you fear for their safety. Every time a child is taken away, regardless of the circumstances, I'm a basket case for weeks. I never get used to it. Each child has left with a piece of my heart.

In addition to being a foster parent, an adoptive parent and a biological parent, I'm also a grammar school teacher. That means I must endure the loss of an entire classroom of children every year! As any teacher will tell you, such a loss can break your heart. Yet, despite the pain, I would never give up the opportunity to nurture a child, no matter how limited the time. It's too precious a gift. This feeling would be tested to the extreme with Billy.

One night, I had an overwhelming feeling that he was going to be leaving very soon. Naturally, I figured this meant that HRS would be taking him to his grandmother. That night, I lifted Billy from his crib, embraced him, sat in the rocking chair and talked to him for a long time. "I don't know if I'll ever see you again in this lifetime, but I will in the next," I promised as we rocked. I wanted the baby to know that he was loved and that I'd always have a place for him in my heart. I gently laid him down to sleep and returned to my bed.

The next morning, my fourteen-year-old daughter, Amber, came running into our room. She was hysterical. She had gone in to cover Billy up and found him stiff, with one eye locked open. I ran to the crib, touched him, rolled him over, then fell to pieces. I called 911, but didn't make any sense. I don't know what came out of my mouth. By then, Amber had calmed down so she took the phone and talked to the dispatcher. The woman advised that we try CPR. My brain finally kicked in and I administered the CPR, but it didn't help. Billy was gone. He had died sometime after I put him to sleep.

The paramedics came and we all went to the hospital. They quickly ruled him dead on arrival. Even though this wasn't my own child, I can't imagine feeling any worse. I was in shock for nearly a week. Amber took it hard as well. She slept with us for the next three or four days. She was afraid to fall asleep, because she continued to be haunted by the image of Billy with one eye open.

As if all this wasn't bad enough, there was, naturally, an extensive HRS investigation. That was scary. You never know how those things will turn out. We were interviewed right at the hospital. Then, when we arrived home, there were a handful of HRS and OSI (Office of Special Investigations) officials waiting to have at us again. To make matters worse, our other foster child was swept away and placed in another foster home for a week, until we were proven innocent of any wrongdoing. The HRS investigators later showed up unannounced at Amber's school and interrogated her on her version of what happened. The coroner ruled the cause of death was SIDS—Sudden Infant Death Syndrome—which cleared our names.

After the fog and nervousness cleared, I began thinking about my last moment with Billy. I feel that the Lord decided that he had suffered enough and knew what was in store for him in the future. This is why I had such an overpowering premonition that night and why I left my bed and spent that special moment with him.

I haven't had many really obvious spiritual things happen to me in my life, but this one definitely was from the beyond. I know that sounds so hokey, especially considering I'm the practical type that doesn't dwell on such things. That's why I have shared this story with very few people. Despite my subsequent pain, I've taken great comfort in the fact that I was able to give both Billy and myself that special moment of maternal bonding before he moved on to a better place. Thankfully, the experience, heartbreaking as it was, hasn't stopped me from reaching out to other children in every possible way.

– Gaye Parnell

Premonitions of a child's death can be profoundly and frighteningly disturbing. Martha Johnson had an inexplicable connection to her son long after the umbilical cord was severed. Not only did she sense the moment of his death, but she was also extremely receptive to his after death contacts as well.

Kevin was my son, my friend, my world. He loved fishing, water sports, life, laughter and God. People naturally gravitated toward him. He was the kind of person who people came to when they needed advice—or just someone to talk to who would listen. He even befriended an elderly lady and used to have tea with her on a regular basis. Kevin didn't even like tea, but would sip it to be polite while he talked with the lonely woman for hours. He was such a nice, caring child who loved helping people. Whenever he saw homeless people, he always gave them money. I used to tell him that not everyone on the street is really homeless and he shouldn't give his money indiscriminately to them. That advice fell on deaf ears. He continued to give his hard earned cash away to anyone with his or her hand out. He'd often give away everything he had on him. When we discussed this, he'd say I didn't trust people enough. I countered that he trusted them too much!

It was probably Kevin's strong, born-again Christian background that made him so generous. He was unbending in his confidence that when he died, he was going to heaven. For that reason, he never feared death.

Kevin usually spent whatever money he didn't give away on his car. He enjoyed working on automobiles, especially the beautiful, yellow 1966 Ford Mustang that he completely restored. That was his pride and joy.

In general, Kevin simply loved life. He lived everyday to its fullest.

When Kevin was fifteen, I began having horrible nightmares that I would lose him when he turned twenty. The tormenting dreams replayed a couple of times a month for the next five years. Each time I woke from one, I felt this awful, devastating pain and my pillow was wet from my tears. I always jumped out of bed, ran to Kevin's room and touched his forehead. He sometimes woke up and asked me, "What's wrong, Mom?" I never gave him the real answer, instead responding that I was just checking up on him. The dreams never specified how he would die, so I had no way of warning him what dangers to avoid.

On April 3, 1991, I had the dream again. This time it was particularly vivid, especially considering that Kevin had turned twenty two months earlier on February 10. I was so shaken that the following day I walked through the house, stared at all his pictures and asked myself how I could ever survive without him.

At 5:00 P.M. that same afternoon, Kevin left to go fishing with a friend who owned a small boat. Before he walked out the door, he turned, looked over the house, then visibly shuddered. "What's wrong?" I asked, picking up on the disturbing change in his mood.

"Nothing. I love you, Mom," he said. I walked him outside and told him to be careful.

Nearly three hours later, at 7:45 P.M., I felt a sudden
chill. "Something's happened to Kevin," I announced to my
husband. Naturally, my husband didn't take my comment
too seriously. At 9:13 P.M., there was a knock at the front
door. I didn't know who it was, just that he or she was there
to deliver awful news. Instead of answering the door, I ran
inside my closet and hid. My husband tracked me down and
told me I had to come out and talk to the visitors. They
turned out to be sheriff's deputies.

For reasons we'll never know, the boat Kevin was in
overturned in the calm pond. Kevin's friend was wearing
heavy boots and couldn't get out of the water. My son pushed
the young man to safety, then got caught in some thick,
strangling water vegetation that twisted around his arms and
legs and pulled him down. It was a freak accident that took
my boy's life—at 7:45 P.M.

In the first month following his death, I experienced
tremendously dark moments when the reality of knowing
that Kevin was never coming home again hit me square in
the face. I found myself panicking from the sheer agony of
wondering whether I could endure the unrelenting pain.
During those moments, I asked God to just get me through
them. Sometimes, in my anger and grief, I felt God had abandoned me. But looking back, I know I couldn't have made it
through the bleakest times without God's presence in my
life.

To further cope, my husband and I found that we
needed to associate with others who had experienced the
devastation of losing a child. We came across an organization
called "Compassionate Friends" that caters to grieving parents like us. We ended up bonding very closely with a couple
who lost their twenty-year-old daughter in an auto accident

two months before Kevin passed. This has helped. None of us can deal with Christmas anymore, so we've joined this couple every December in Las Vegas, because for us there is no Christmas there.

Kevin's Contacts

It took two long years before I had what I believe to be my first real contact with Kevin. It came in the form of a dream so vivid and overpowering I felt it had to be something more profound and meaningful than a simple dream. I saw Kevin and our new friends' daughter sitting in the most stunning, vibrantly green grass I could ever hope to see. They were talking for a while, then got up to walk away. I tried to get to them, but I couldn't make them aware of my presence or touch their bodies. I heard Kevin ask our friends' daughter, "How can we help our moms? They need to know that we're all right."

"There has to be some way we can reach them," she answered. Shortly afterward, they vanished.

I've since concluded that this brief peek into their world was done to prepare me for the next contact. I dreamed I was at the cemetery sitting in the grass. A hand touched my shoulder. I turned to look and it was Kevin. He had tears in his eyes and asked me, "Mom, why did I have to die?" Not knowing how to answer that, I asked him if he had seen God. The most peaceful look came over his face and the tears dried. "Yes, Mom," he answered.

"What's heaven like?" I asked.

"It's more beautiful than anyone could ever imagine," he told me.

I asked him about God again. "Oh, Mom, he's so wonderful. More wonderful than I could tell you, or than you could ever understand." A few moments later, he hugged and kissed me and said he didn't want to leave but had to go. He was teary once again. When I woke up, I truly felt that Kevin had visited me. It was wonderful—but the fact that he had those tears in his eyes has really bothered me. I don't know what to make of that. Maybe he was sad because of my pain?

In another dream, he told me that even though I couldn't see him, he was with me. He then instructed me to go to his closet and his scent would greet me. I remembered his words when I woke up and immediately went to the closet. The moment I opened the door his distinctive smell was so strong it nearly overwhelmed me.

A few months later, I noticed that one of our antique clocks wasn't working. Shaped like a schoolhouse with the time piece embedded in the front, it had been Kevin's favorite. I had promised to give it to him when I passed on. Checking it closer, I was shocked to see that it was frozen on 7:45. Finding that eerie, I took it in to have it fixed. No one has been able to determine why it broke or was able to get it working again. It remains stopped at 7:45.

On the first anniversary of Kevin's death, we went to the cemetery to pay our respects. The manager informed us that they had to move Kevin's body, because they placed him too far over in the plot. I became unglued at that news. We took the battle to the cemetery's home office in Houston. They were holding all the legal cards and insisted it had to be done. I made them go over, step by step, how it would be accomplished, then got them to agree that a man I trusted from the funeral home along with my brother would be there to oversee the process. I also instructed them not to inform me when they did it.

A few weeks later, I was lying in bed just waking up when I heard Kevin's voice. "Mom, it's over."

"What?" I asked.

"It's over."

I had no idea what he was talking about. I looked at my clock and noticed that it was 8:35 A.M. A half hour later my husband came home from having car repairs done. His eyes were strangely swollen. He sat down next to me and said "It's done." I figured my husband meant his car repairs were done and thought his overly emotional reaction strange. I asked why he was making such a big deal about his car.

"No, I mean it's done," he repeated.

"What's done?"

"Kevin is moved and it was performed with such ease."

"They moved him at 8:35 didn't they?" I asked.

"Yes. How did you know?"

"Kevin came here and told me."

Not long afterward, I was sleeping and heard Kevin's voice in a dream say "Mom, Papaw is going to be leaving soon." I sat straight up in bed and looked at my clock. It was 6:45 A.M. I woke my husband and told him what happened. We quickly dressed and drove to my father's house a few minutes away. My dad, who had been ailing and was eighty-three, died shortly after we arrived at 7:10 A.M. Thanks to Kevin, we were able to be with him when he passed over.

When I had one of my surgeries for urethral diverticulum, a rare and painful disorder, I saw Kevin just as I was about to lose consciousness from the anesthesia. He was at the door smiling and waving, then walked through it and left. Since he made a point of showing me that he wasn't staying around, I took that to mean that my operation was going to be successful and I wouldn't be going to heaven with him then.

Because of these contacts, I no longer fear death. I believe death is just a crossing to somewhere else, a place where there are no more pain or tears. That will be especially nice, because before Kevin's death, I never imagined how many tears could be inside me.

– Martha Johnson

Though Bonnie Blankenship's premonition did not pinpoint specific details about her son's death, it was still powerful enough to frighten her. As she relates in the next story, she knew the moment she said goodbye to her son that she'd never see him alive again.

When he was born, Michael Allen Howe weighed in at ten pounds, nine ounces. It was February 28, 1970, and from that moment on I knew I had myself a handful. He was a terrific baby, hardly ever cried and was extraordinarily brave. The child knew no fear. He ran instead of walked, leaped head first into any challenging new experience and wanted to squeeze every drop out of every single day of his life.

Early on, Michael developed a special affinity for anything to do with water. Swimming, boating, fishing, diving, skiing, surfing—if it made him wet, he wanted to try it. Beginning when he was twenty, for three years, Mike and his pals planned a dream trip to Costa Rica and Panama where they would enjoy the pristine surrounding waters. Mike worked part time, mowed yards and even sold his car to raise the money to go on the summer long adventure. Finally, everything was set.

As the departure date approached, I began feeling apprehensive about his trip. My increasing anxiety was fueled in part by simple mother's instincts. I just knew something bad was going to happen in Central America. This sense of foreboding was intensified by the signals I was receiving from Mike himself. For weeks, he and his friends talked in odd, fatalistic riddles about "Babylon," which he explained was their code word for "the time we have on earth." He followed this with a series of totally uncharacteristic acts that led me to believe he had no intention of returning home. Shortly before he left, he abruptly broke off his relationship with his girlfriend of three years. His only explanation was that it "would be for the best." A close friend came by the house to help him pack. The friend found a red tie and asked Mike what to do with it. "Keep it," Mike replied. "You're going to need it." He followed that cryptic statement by taking an unusual interest in various family photographs, often staring at pictures for a long time while deep in thought. When I asked Mike about it, he replied that he wanted to remember what everyone looked like.

On Mother's Day, 1993, Mike presented me with a peach tree sapling, planted it, then continued preparing for his trip. When he was all set to go, we hugged in the kitchen and he assured me once again that he would be fine. I tried to be strong, but I couldn't help breaking down and crying. I knew in my heart that I would never see my son again. I also knew that no matter how strongly I felt about something bad happening, I wasn't going to be able to stop him from going. Sensing my deep fear, Mike held me in his big arms and rocked me back and forth like I did to him when he was a child. "It's going to be okay," he kept saying.

"No, it won't!" I shot back. "No, it won't!" I couldn't take it anymore and left for work, crying the whole way.

That evening, when I returned home, I walked into my other son's room and nearly went into shock. Of all Mike's worldly possessions, he treasured his skateboard and favorite yellow hat the most. He frequently warned his little brother, then five, not to touch either one. Yet the skateboard and hat were now in my younger son's room, leaning against his night stand.

At first, everything seemed to be going perfectly in Central America. Mike called often from Costa Rica, bubbling with news about the beautiful water, the wonderful people, the strange and exotic towns and everything else he and his friends were experiencing. I had to admit, it sounded like paradise. "It sounds like you're in heaven," I observed.

"Yeah, Mom, I think I am!"

In Panama, the three young adventurers shared a little hut that cost them a mere $4 a day. It consisted of four walls, cut out windows and no door. They slept in hammocks and lived off the land, dining on fruit and coconuts—and they still thought they were in heaven.

On July 13, 1993, Mike and his friends hopped out of their rope beds at 3:00 A.M., grabbed hold of their surfboards and headed for the ocean to catch the early morning tide. To get to an isolated beach that promised a memorable series of monster waves, the young men had to walk for miles through the jungles of Panama.

Undeterred, they made it without incident and surfed for most of the day. One friend got tired and headed back to the hut to rest. Mike and his other friend stayed in the water. Always pushing the limits, Mike had an idea. Pointing to a huge mountain that loomed over the ocean, he said, "Hey, lets go over the mountain and surf where nobody's ever surfed before!" Mike's friend thought it was a swell idea, so off they went. The two young men tackled the mountain—decked in swim trunks and boots and carrying their surf boards. As they neared the top, Mike started crisscrossing a bit and walked toward the side of the mountain instead of straight up. His friend warned him that it was dangerous to do it that way, but Mike wouldn't hear of it. "I got it," he said. Mike's friend turned, walked five more steps and reached the peak of the mountain. The next thing he heard was Mike's yell. My son had lost his footing and tumbled down the mountain into the warm salt water and angry, crashing waves.

At first, his friend couldn't even find Mike. The water was rough and the rocks were jagged and threatening. Mike's friend ran down the slope the best he could and finally found Mike floating in the water. Mike was conscious, but badly hurt. His friend struggled for an hour to get Mike out of that dangerous nook, fighting the violent waves, sucking riptides and tricky swirls of water. Finally reaching shore, he determined that Mike's arm and leg were fractured, among other injuries. He ripped up both his and Mike's shirts and tied Mike's battered limbs in makeshift splints. "My mom's going to be so mad at me," my son said, gritting his teeth through the pain.

His friend left Mike on his surfboard and went running for help. They were so far from civilization that the friend quickly grew concerned for Mike's welfare and came back. By then, Mike was fading fast. His friend held Mike as he passed over to the next world.

As tough as this has been on me—and there are no adequate words to describe it—there have been some positives that came out of this tragedy. A campaign in Mike's memory raised more than $10,000 for the marine biology department of his college, the University of North Carolina at Wilmington. Two scholarships were started in Mike's name to enable students to attend a special summer leadership conference. His former high school collected $4,000 in Mike's name and used it to support the Student Council Association.

One of my most far reaching accomplishments has been starting an organization called "M.O.M.s"—Motivated On-Line Moms. This began as an E-mail loop of grieving mothers trading encouraging notes back and forth over the World Wide Web. It has grown into a full-fledged support organization that holds meetings and retreats in various cities and operates a popular web page [see Appendix A]. The interaction between us moms has been a tremendous comfort to us all. So many of the mothers have reached out to each other where before each grieved inwardly and alone. It helps to have special shoulders to cry on—shoulders belonging to a person who has been where you are.

Mike's Contacts

Three months after the accident, I was sitting at my kitchen table, writing thank you notes to people who had been kind, drinking coffee and mostly crying. Mike came up behind me like a whisper. I knew instantly it was him and I sensed that if I tried to reach out and touch him, I wouldn't be able to connect. He moved to my side, kissed me on the cheek, smiled and floated out the open kitchen window. I sat there and cried for hours, sobbing so hard.

Mike has not come back to see me since. I am sure it's because I hurt him by crying so much. Though I'd like to see him again, I'm thankful to have had the chance to say good-bye.

– Bonnie Blankenship

As the previous stories have shown, premonitions of one's child's death can be very disturbing and frightening. The premonitions are similar to after death contacts because of their paranormal nature, however, the similarities end there. The contacts, as the various stories reveal, do not elicit fear and horror like the premonitions. For most parents, the contacts are consoling images that provide brief but tender moments with lost children. These moments are often the only chance children and their parents get to bid each other a final farewell.

Chapter Eight

Tearful Departures,
Tender Mercies

Not everyone's contact with his or her lost child is dramatic and earth shattering. Some are just brief, small moments, like an unusual thought, a sudden feeling or a brief dream. Yet, even these can be tremendously comforting and affirming. Plus, you can never underestimate the healing power even the smallest incident can have upon a bereaved parent.

My son, Bradley Cooper Moore, seemed to collect nicknames like other boys collect baseball cards. He was tall and thin with long arms and, when he rode his skateboard and flapped his arms to stay balanced, his friends would say, "You look like a bird, man!" Thus he became known as "Birdman." At various times his friends also called him "Bird" and "Seymour" (for C. Moore).

Brad was my youngest child and only son. Our personalities clicked from day one. We were soul mates, as well as mother and son. He was just like Will Rogers—he never met a person he didn't like. Brad was a friend to everybody, young, old and in between. In school, he defied typecasting because he hung out with scholars, athletes, "rockers," "skaters" and even those kids labeled "losers." In Brad's eyes, there were no losers. He could always find worth in someone, no matter how reclusive or socially inept he or she was. Brad wasn't perfect and certainly wasn't an angel, but he had a special zest for life, living each hour as if it were his last.

The day before his eighteenth birthday, September 2, 1989, he made plans to meet with some friends, go to the river and spend the day celebrating. After visiting his grandmother, Brad headed home in his pickup truck to prepare for the river excursion. A motorcycle cut him off at an interchange, causing Brad to swerve and lose control of his vehicle. His truck nicked the back of a motor home, spun around and hit the motorcycle, causing the two-wheeled vehicle to slide under his truck. Brad's vehicle continued to spin out of control to such an extent that his front wheels reared up and pulled the truck off the highway, plunging it into a thirty-five feet deep cement flood control gully. His truck was such a tangle of twisted steel that he had to be removed with the jaws of life. The motorcycle driver, a young man in his late twenties, died at the scene.

At the hospital, they were able to "jump-start" Brad's body, but his brain was dead. Though Brad would not survive, he was able to be an organ donor. Although his heart and lungs were too damaged to be used, the surgeons were able to successfully transplant his kidneys, liver, eyes, skin and bone. The vibrant parts of my son's young body ended up helping forty-two other lives. Ironically, he gave this gift of life on his own birthday.

For me, there was paralyzing grief afterward. I miss everything about him, even the not-so-perfect things he did. Most of all I miss the laughter. He was the laughter in my life.

Six weeks after Brad's death, my husband and I joined a support group called Compassionate Friends. Eight months later, when the chapter leader retired, I found myself taking the position. I stayed on the job for eight years, until 1997, when I was forced to fight my own battle against lung cancer—a successful but draining process that included surgery. I'm still very active with the group, taking phone calls day and night, editing a monthly newsletter and planning many activities. Our organization has since joined forces with a similar group—Bereaved Parents USA—and together, we have expanded our operations further. We take phone calls from individuals and families who have lost a child. We also receive referrals from hospitals, police departments, doctors and counselors who are trying to help grieving families. In addition to this, I've spoken at hospitals and other facilities to promote awareness of the Southern California Organ Procurement program. Through these speaking engagements, I've helped to make the public aware of the constant and growing need for organ donors and I've convinced people to sign donor cards. By pouring myself into this worthwhile volunteer work, I am coping with the loss of my "soul mate."

I've learned many things since Brad's death, the most important of which is the need to be open-minded. I've become receptive to the magic of all the little things in life. I view everything in a new light and appreciate the smallest of life's gifts. In return, my gift back to the world is reaching out to families who are just starting on the long, hard path through grief.

Sometimes, when I get weary, I think that it might be time for me to get away from it all, pass the baton to another person and have someone else handle the phones. Then I'll receive a call from a person who is in so much pain, hurting so badly, so desperate to receive the slightest hope. I'm able to help them, comfort them and get them through the night. I've realized that this is my calling and I can't walk away from it. I need to be there for these people the way others were there for me.

Brad's Contacts

I've been blessed with many visits in a variety of ways from Brad since he died. Most have come in the form of strange and unusual dreams. A few of the most powerful were transmitted through other people—some of whom weren't even close friends.

A few days after Brad died, I dreamed I was in the hospital with him. He got out of bed, stood up, walked toward the door and disappeared into the hallway. Although I didn't know where he was going or what he was doing, I followed him through the exit. Suddenly, I felt like Dorothy in *The Wizard of Oz*. We were in an incredible place that had colors I had never experienced before and plants, trees and flowers of a vividness and beauty I had never imagined. Brad stood there smiling, telling me he was fine. Then the vision began to fade until it was gone. I believe that this was Brad's way of telling me he was okay, that he was in a beautiful place and he would be around when I needed him.

I've had many other dreams, but the next really memorable contact came when I was awake. I was in Brad's room, lying on his bed with the door closed. I started drifting off, but I was not yet asleep when I felt a presence in the room. I became afraid, thinking it was a stranger or a burglar. Then I remembered that Brad's door made a lot of noise whenever it was opened, so I knew I would have heard an intruder trying to enter. So I laid there motionless, my eyes still closed, and soon felt the most wonderful sensation. Although the sensation I experienced is difficult to describe, it would be best understood by the following explanation: if a person takes her hand, places it very close to her cheek—but not touching the cheek—then moves the hand as if to caress her cheek, that's what I felt; a "heavenly caress." It was incredible! I knew it was Brad. After that, I felt the sensation all over my body—as if he was giving me a "heavenly hug." I wanted to open my eyes and see him, but somehow I knew that if I did, Brad would vanish. I waited for a few more seconds, then couldn't stand not looking any longer and decided to take a peek. When I opened my eyes, I saw nothing and the sensation immediately stopped. As brief as that "heavenly caress" was and as long ago as it occurred, I can still feel it as if it were yesterday.

Several acquaintances have had dreams about Brad and strangely enough, they all have had the same exact dream. In the dream, Brad always asks them to tell me that he is fine, that he is not in pain or frightened and he didn't suffer during the accident. He always specifically states that he was "only a little scared" right before the accident. Every person who has had the dream has told me that Brad spoke those same exact words: "only a little scared."

– Linda Moore

Even when a contact is made through an acquaintance, the impact on the lost child's parent is still powerful. Yet it is the direct contact, no matter how fleeting or seemingly inconsequential, that seems to provide the most solace and healing for a grief-stricken mother or father. Rose Stenrose discusses in the next story how a brief dream and a shooting star were sufficient reminders for her family that her son, Keith, lives on.

I lost my dear son, Keith, on November 22, 1998. He was twenty-seven years old, married and had two children—a ten-month old baby and a son that wasn't born yet. He was a nice, quiet man with dark blonde hair and an easygoing personality. He was skilled with his hands and worked as a master mechanic.

Keith was killed by a hit-and-run driver while walking across a street. We are still trying to find out the truth about what exactly happened that night, but so far we've been unsuccessful. Losing him to a hit-and-run accident, where there are no answers, has been especially painful.

When Keith died, I was devastated. I started searching for answers to help me deal with this horrible pain. I had delved into the subject of the afterlife to some extent when my mother passed ten years before, so I had some familiarity with it. After Keith was killed, I naturally began to pursue this subject with a greater passion. I searched the web for information and have read many books on the afterlife. This research, along with my own personal experiences, has convinced me without a doubt that after death, life goes on in a different form and that we can break down the barriers between this world and the next to reconnect with our lost loved ones.

Keith's Contacts

My contacts from Keith have mostly come after I've prayed for them. The first was a very real dream that seemed so different from typical dreams. In it, Keith came to me and said "Mom, I'm happy. I feel great!" I was relieved to see he looked as healthy and joyful as he had been in life.

The next contact was when I was alone on Mother's Day. I was sitting in the kitchen when I suddenly heard Keith's voice as clear as day: "Happy Mother's Day, Mom. I love you."

Another brief contact came one night when I woke up and saw Keith in solid form leaving my bedside. I felt such peace and comfort and went right back to sleep.

My daughter has also received contacts. The first one came when she was grocery shopping. She wandered into the book section, saw a bright purple book and felt compelled to reach for it. She opened the book to a random page and was shocked to see the words: "Your brother is in heaven and happy." She closed the book and cried happy tears for the peace those words brought to her.

On my daughter's birthday, she was feeling especially sad about Keith's death. After leaving our house, she went home and prayed that Keith would send her another sign and wish her a happy birthday. She then went out to her front porch and saw her first shooting star! She's convinced that this was Keith's way of answering her birthday wish.

– Rose Stenrose

Life moves so quickly and can be taken away in an instant. When tragedy strikes, small moments of warmth and peace can make the loss of a child easier to bear, because the parents can cherish these contacts, however brief, forever. Sheri Tabler tells such a story.

On Sunday, July 20, 1997, my son Jeremy was struck by a car while riding his bike. He was just eight years old. He wasn't wearing his helmet, but the accident was so severe it probably wouldn't have made a difference. On Monday, July 21, it was determined that he was brain dead.

As I sat at the hospital waiting for the doctors to determine if there was any hope, I knew in my heart that Jeremy was already gone. I realized I had a choice to make—whether or not to donate his organs. As I sat there and considered everything, it seemed only natural to let Jeremy live on in the bodies of others. When I made that decision, I suddenly felt a sense of peace that I'd never experienced before.

Jeremy's corneas, liver, heart and kidneys were used. I was extremely surprised that both kidneys were used, because one had been damaged in the accident. That made me realize how great a need there must be for organs—even ones that aren't perfect.

After the transplant surgeries had taken place, I spoke with the recovery counselor and she told me, "Every one of the recipients is doing better than expected." I thought that was truly wonderful. To date, I've heard from the liver and heart recipients. The woman who received Jeremy's liver was fifty-three at the time and the heart recipient was fourteen. Both told me that they're doing extremely well. In fact, the teenager who received Jeremy's heart was preparing to go on his first camping trip. The teen seemed so excited to be able to do things that he had never been able to do before. I know that Jeremy would be proud that he has made such a difference in so many peoples' lives.

Because of the donation program, I was able to answer the prayers of others through my tragedy and Jeremy was given the opportunity to create miracles for others.

Jeremy's Contacts

When I arrived home from the hospital after Jeremy died, I lit a religious candle and placed his picture on the mantel. As I sat there and looked at his picture, the most amazing thing I've ever seen occurred. A bright halo of light formed around his head in the picture. It gave me such a sense of warmth and comfort. It was then I knew my little angel son was on his way to heaven into the arms of God.

– Sheri Tabler

Even when a child has an incredibly short time on earth, it is a blessing for a parent. Though the relationship they share in life may be short, as the next story tells, their love can live on after death.

My husband and I were married for seven years before I finally became pregnant. We were both so happy. The ultrasound revealed that it was going to be a girl, so we had the name all picked out—Joanna Jean Bruner. She was due on February 28, 1996.

Like most expectant mothers, I immediately busied myself with plans and purchases for our new baby. I even cross-stitched a quilt. On the night that I completed the quilt, I started feeling sick and went to bed early. I woke up at 5:00 A.M. in terrible pain and had to be rushed to the hospital. The doctors performed an emergency caesarean section to give Joanna a shot at life. It was only November 5; she was nearly four months premature.

Joanna was born that night weighing only one pound, four ounces. She fought valiantly, but lived for only a day. Despite that tiny life span, I still miss her terribly. A child is your child no matter how brief her existence.

This experience has made me aware that we never know what tomorrow will bring, so I've learned to cherish every moment. It has bonded me closer than ever to my husband. It's taught me how to help others in their grief. In fact, I've started a chapter of the bereaved parents support group, Compassionate Friends, in my hometown of Louisville, Kentucky. By helping others, I've helped myself.

Joanna's Contacts

Since Joanna's death, I have had numerous strange and wondrous contacts that have followed the same theme. The most vivid was when I woke up one night and saw a young girl, about three years old, bathed in a warm light hovering above me near the ceiling. She didn't speak aloud, but I heard her talking in my mind. She told me, *Hello, Mom. I'm okay. I'm waiting for you.* Though I never got to see Joanna grow to be a toddler, I'm sure it was her.

I've seen Joanna in a number of dreams as well. She always smiles and tells me she's okay. I feel that this is my baby's way of reaching out to me.

– Susan Bruner

Seeing a child struggle with physical limitations and illnesses is heartrending for a parent. In some cases, death may be a blessing in disguise for the child, but that knowledge does little to diminish a parent's anguish. As the next story relates, solace comes with the realization that in the afterlife, the child has the gifts she didn't in this life: good health, happiness and the ability to walk, run and play.

Amanda was a beautiful baby. I loved her so much. In my eyes, she was just perfect. My mother-in-law noticed that Amanda had a weak cry and suspected something was wrong, but held her tongue. I hadn't been around a lot of babies, so I didn't know enough to tell whether Amanda's cry was normal or not.

I did notice that at two months she still couldn't pick up her head when lying on her stomach. The doctors said she was just lazy, but as time passed, the situation didn't improve. After a series of test, the doctors determined that Amanda had Spinal Muscular Atrophy II, a serious ailment that kills the anterior horn cells and erodes a child's physical abilities. We were told that she would never be able to walk. The sudden news was devastating. When we got over the shock, we became determined to do anything and everything to insure that Amanda's life would be as pleasant as possible.

Despite her problems, Amanda was a happy baby who loved music and singing. She even tried to dance in her little seat. We bought videos that showed children singing and she was thrilled, believing that they were performing just for her.

Amanda's condition deteriorated to the point that at eighteen months old, she could no longer eat. Instead, she slept—from Wednesday until Saturday morning, June 1. When she briefly woke up, I knew it was over. She was just tired of the fight. She looked at us, said goodbye with her eyes, closed them and moved on to a better world.

I am no longer the same person I was before Amanda was born. I don't take life for granted and don't let petty things bother me. For any parent who has lost a child, my advice is to talk about it, cry when you want and when it all seems too overwhelming, just get out of the house. That's the best medicine.

Amanda's Contacts

My niece was born two weeks before Amanda died. When she was a month old and visiting us, we heard faint music coming from the room where she was napping. The song we heard was "Twinkle, Twinkle Little Star." I went to the room to investigate where the music was coming from, but I discovered that my niece was fast asleep and the music had stopped. After I left the room, the music started again. This happened over and over. I was totally perplexed. The music sounded like it was coming from a child's toy. Determined to figure out where the music was coming from, I went back into the room for a thorough search. This time, the baby was awake, laughing and staring behind me as if she was watching somebody. I turned around and headed in the direction where my niece was staring and I finally discovered that the music had come from a baby rattle that played "Twinkle, Twinkle Little Star" at the press of a button. I tried to get the song to play again by pushing the button, but the rattle didn't seem to work. After I put it back down, the rattle started playing on its own again. I was truly baffled. When the toy finally stopped, a different song, "It's a Small World," started playing in Amanda's room. I traced the melody to a toy box and I began digging through the toys to locate the source. When I finally did, I realized it was another one of Amanda's musical rattles. I knew then that it was Amanda behind all the music. She was really being playful that day. Before she passed away, Amanda never even had the strength to push the buttons to make the rattles play music. I think she was just letting me know that she could now run and play from room to room, doing things she could never do in life.

– Sue Harris

Small contacts from a lost child are enough to begin filling the hole in a grieving parent's heart. Even though he was tremendously physically challenged throughout his short life, Betsy Watson's son, Luke, was the light of her life. After he passed, he let her know in small ways that he would continue to be her light.

Luke's heart stopped for several minutes when he was born. It was a touch and go situation, but the doctors got it beating again. That close call was the first indication that he was born with severe handicaps. He never developed much physically. Mentally, we were never sure how much he understood. We do know he experienced hunger, anger, excitement, fear, laughter—and that he had a family that loved him dearly. Most people who met Luke were amazed by his beautiful blue eyes and his cheery smile that wouldn't quit. An admiring friend described Luke's long eyelashes as "paint brushes."

Nothing came easy for our little buddy. Luke had to be fed through a tube and struggled to hold up his head. He had great difficulty moving his arms and legs, so we moved them for him. Luke required hip surgery at nine months and again at five years. Through it all, he was such a little trooper. He lit up my world every time he smiled.

My son only spoke one time, saying "Mommy." That was such a thrill for me, but it's even more amazing how many things a person can convey without using words. I learned to pick up on all his needs through expressions, mannerisms and little noises.

Most of all, my son taught me how to love by showing me his love everyday. Luke made his family realize how beautiful life is and how much we take for granted. He also brought out the best in his older sisters. They embraced the challenge of a "differently-abled" little brother and helped me so much with Luke's care. My daughters have spoken publicly about their experiences, helping others understand that a person shouldn't be judged by what he can or cannot do, but by who he is. My daughters see the person first, not the handicap. How wonderful it would be if everyone could be so open-minded and accepting of others.

I have also learned that I have the greatest husband in the world. He is the best father Luke and the girls could ever have. We were all a team and we still are. My husband and I laugh today when we think about how traumatic it was to have to wake up in the middle of the night to take care of our girls when they were infants, when with Luke, there were nights when two hours of sleep was all we had.

Luke succumbed to his many physical problems when he was five years, six months and twenty-eight days old. Despite the constant care he required, we were devastated by his passing. I would never have anticipated hurting so much. Another mother of a disabled child had told me when Luke was born that I was being forced into a much smaller world.

Well, when Luke died, I was forced into an even smaller world.

I talk about Luke all the time. It feels good to me to do so, even if it makes others uncomfortable. He is still a part of my world, part of me. I love him more everyday.

Luke's Contacts

On the morning of Luke's funeral, I woke up and immediately became alarmed because I couldn't hear Luke's breathing from the baby monitor. I had momentarily forgotten that he had passed away. When I came to my senses, I looked across the room to the spot on the dresser where we had kept the baby monitor and noticed that in its place was a tiny, glowing red light. I walked over to the dresser to get a closer look and discovered that it was the miniature lantern on my key chain. It had never been turned on before. In fact, I didn't even know it worked! The moment I touched the light, it went out. The next morning, it was back on. Again, when I touched it, it went off. That little light greeted me for six mornings in a row following the funeral. It was as if Luke was saying to me, *I am with you even though you can no longer touch me. I will continue to light up your world.*

– Betsy Watson

The belief in a higher power and that a deceased child is in heaven is comforting for most parents. In the next story, Barbara Velard is not only happy her son is with God, but is also appreciative of God for allowing her time on earth with her wonderful son. With so much going for him in life and so much ahead of him to be accomplished, Dylon Velard's death was very hard for his family. Yet he has let them know he lives on and has even looked after his family in their times of need.

Dylon was an accomplished saxophone player and a member of both his high school's jazz band and marching band. He was also in the process of teaching himself to play the oboe, because he felt he had a better chance of earning a college scholarship if he had that more unusual ability.

Aside from his love of music, Dylon was active in the drama club. He didn't particularly enjoy being the center of attention, so he worked backstage building scenery and props. He was always helpful to others and during one school production, he whispered words of encouragement from behind a prop to a young actress suffering from stage fright.

As a boy scout, Dylon went on many camping trips and hikes, yet still found time to do volunteer work at our church, help with the music at Sunday services and participate in the church youth group.

When a close friend of ours struggled through a difficult pregnancy, Dylon frequently went over to her house to fix her lunch, play games and just keep her company. The poor woman ended up losing her babies and Dylon, so sensitive and caring, took the woman's loss very hard, because he felt so close to her.

On February 6, 1995, jazz band practice let out early. It was a bitter, cold night—fourteen degrees—and a friend offered Dylon a ride home. He agreed, because otherwise, he would have had to wait twenty minutes in the cold until his father arrived. It had snowed the day before and the roads were icy. The driver lost control on a curve just as he was leaving the school. A truck slammed into the vehicle on my son's side. Dylon suffered massive head injuries and never regained consciousness. We stayed with him at the hospital for a week until the Lord took him home. He was only fourteen years old.

I can't express how great a loss it's been. My son was a very special person. His adult life would have been a good and productive one. He would have given to this world so much more than he took, but now he will never have the opportunity to do so.

The years have passed and the pain has not gone away. Will I ever be able to think of Dylon without crying? I don't know, but I will always praise the Lord for having given us the fourteen years we had with Dylon. Our son taught us so much about life and love. His father and I were so proud of the young man he had become. We will always cherish Dylon's memory.

Dylon's Contacts

On Wednesday night, February 8, while Dylon was still unconscious in the hospital, the pressure in his brain elevated and the nurses told us that the end was near. I sensed that his spirit left his body at that moment, even though his body was being kept alive. At the same time, my husband was home sleeping. He had a dream that Dylon came to see him and told him, "Daddoo, I'm okay. Please don't worry about me." Across town, two of my friends had similar dreams. In them, Dylon told them, "Tell my mom and dad that I'm okay and not to worry about me."

The next day at the hospital, my daughter was standing next to Dylon's bed, holding his hand, while my husband and I sat in chairs on the other side of the bed. My daughter suddenly became wide-eyed and told us she saw Dylon and a very short man standing behind us. I asked her to describe the man. She did and I realized it was her grandfather, whom she never really knew. Dylon, however, had been very close to his grandfather. I knew then that Dylon's grandfather had come to take Dylon and allowed Dylon's little sister to experience the passing. That has been a great comfort to us all.

On November 30, 1999, I had to have serious emergency surgery for a perforated stomach. I came close to dying. When I was in the recovery room, my family came to visit. I don't remember much about the visit, because I was heavily sedated. I do remember opening my eyes and seeing four people looking at me. Two were smiling and two were crying. One looked like Dylon. I thought I was dreaming. The next day, the doctor said he met my three children. "You must be mistaken. I only have one daughter and one son now. You must have thought my husband was one of my children."

"I know your husband," the doctor assured me. "There were two boys and a young girl here visiting." My husband just looked at me and smiled. "It must have been Dylon checking up on you," he said.

– Barbara Velard

Sometimes it takes the death of a loved one for a person to realize how much he or she should value of life. Beth Russell is amazed by her loving son's small, but touching, after death contacts and appreciates how losing one family member has drawn those left behind closer to each other.

My husband and I tried for five years to have children, with no luck. Then we had three in a span of two years and eight months! After a son and daughter, Casey was our last child. He was born on Friday, January 13, 1984. For some, that might be considered a bad omen, but I thought it was neat. I was born on a Friday the 13th myself!

Casey was an easy-going boy who was always smiling and freely offered hugs and kisses to everyone. He was such an unusually loving boy. His teachers often told us how much they enjoyed his warmth and wonderful smile.

Our kids grew up in a good neighborhood filled with children playing up and down the streets. When Casey wasn't joining in the fun, he was off hunting with his father and older brother or down at the park playing Little League baseball.

On Father's Day, 1994, Casey invited his good friend, Adam, to spend the night with him. Adam was eleven and Casey was ten. The next day, after watching some television, the two became restless and wanted to go outside. They decided to explore nearby train tracks. The pair ended up on a railroad trestle built over a creek. As they were looking down from the trestle into the water, a freight train with eighty-two cars came thundering around a curve. The trestle was enclosed with steel walls. The boys had no escape. The conductor and others on the train reported that in his panic, Adam caught his foot between two cross ties and Casey spent his last seconds trying to pull his friend free.

We had a double funeral with a tremendous turnout. It was a nice tribute to two fine boys. They were both so well-liked in the community. The boys were buried in adjoining plots and are now forever in our hearts.

From my experience, I've learned that grief can be very different for a husband and wife. Men sometimes think they have to have an answer for everything. I finally told my husband, Frank, that I didn't want or expect answers, I just needed him to listen. Luckily, he understood. There are a lot of couples who can't do this. It's just too hard to be there for each other when you're in so much pain. Sometimes, one has to find a friend or family member to talk to instead of one's spouse.

After Casey died, I was so consumed with grief that I wasn't there for my other children. At the time, I didn't realize it, but I do now and I regret the mistakes I made. I've tried hard, since coming to that realization, to be there for my children. We all try to get through each day together.

I've found help and healing by reaching out to others who have lost a child. When you've been through something like that, it's important to let people know that it is possible to survive when you don't feel you can or even want to. The best way I've done this is by joining a group of bereaved parents on the Internet called "M.O.M.s." Since doing this, I've also started my own home business. It's a line of greeting cards that can be ordered on the Internet. The greeting cards are another way I keep Casey's memory alive. This, I feel, is the function of survivors. I want everyone to know that Casey is still important in our lives, just like my other two children. They are what kept my husband and I going. I thank God for them. Losing a child has made me realize just what a gift my other children are and how they should be treasured.

Casey's Contacts

My contacts have been brief and simple, but very meaningful to me. I went to the cemetery a few months after Casey died to brush the leaves and other debris from his headstone. After I finished, I was sitting there thinking about how much I would have loved at that moment to kiss his perpetually chapped lips. As I was thinking this, a drop of dew hit me square in the lips. I knew it was Casey's way of giving me a kiss.

Another time, I was in bed one night thinking about what to do with all of Casey's things. I was wondering if I should give his friend some of Casey's baseball equipment.

"Is that what you want me to do, Casey?" I asked aloud, searching for an answer. The moment I finished my question, the train whistle blew. I believe, because of the manner in which he died, the train whistle was Casey's way of giving me an answer. I took it to mean yes.

– Beth Russell

Even having just days or weeks with a child in this life is more than enough time for a parent to bond with the child and subsequently grieve for the child's loss. Small contacts afterward, as the next story tells, give peace and comfort, allowing the loving relationship to continue even longer.

Jack was born prematurely, just twenty-five weeks into my pregnancy. He weighed one pound, twelve ounces, which was actually big for a child born that early. Of course, he was still very, very tiny. He fought hard to survive and impressed the nurses with how feisty he was. He loved to raise his middle finger when he slept, turning a gesture usually considered profane into a curious and amusing habit.

Though he was with us for only two weeks, he changed our lives forever. He taught me how to be strong in the face of trials, because even with the odds stacked against him, he tried hard to be strong. His short life taught me to be more compassionate toward others no matter what the circumstances. He also helped me realize in what direction I want my life to go.

My family has had a hard time dealing with Jack's death. My oldest son, Josh, who was eight years old at the time, went right to school from the hospital the morning Jack died of pneumonia on September 28, 1995. Josh kissed his brother's lifeless body goodbye then silently went on his way, his emotions locked inside him. As time has passed, he is learning how to talk about his feelings a little more. My daughter, then five, has learned from Jack's death to love and appreciate her brothers. Even when she gets frustrated with her big brother, as little sisters often do, she thinks of Jack and her frustration usually goes away. She is very sensitive and misses Jack very much. She talks about him all the time. My husband has difficulty discussing Jack at all. I'm not sure that he will ever be able to talk about Jack. Our youngest son, Jeremy, nearly two, kisses Jack's picture every night before he goes to bed. When we ask him where Jack is, Jeremy points up to heaven.

I want my children to know it is good to talk about and remember Jack, even if he wasn't with us very long.

Jack's Contacts

Jack was so small, he remained in intensive care his entire life. I was never able to hold him like a mother needs to until after he died. In the days following his death, I prayed that God would bring Jack back. It was silly, I know, but I just wanted to hold my son and hug him one time. One day, as I lay down for a nap, the Lord gave me the most wonderful gift. He sent Jack to me. Jack reached his little arms around my neck and squeezed me so tightly. He whispered in my ear, "Love you, Momma." I thought at first I was dreaming, but then I realized I'd never fallen asleep! My eyes were open the whole time. I am so thankful for that one hug, even though I'd like to have more. It was the most incredible feeling I've ever experienced. I thank God for giving me the gift I so desperately wanted and needed. As the saying goes, "God gets us out of very little, but he gets us through everything." I have taken those words to heart.

– Amy Hooyer

Jack Hooyer's visitation to his mother, though brief, is an experience which has affected the rest of her life positively. For Lynn Rosecrans, the tragic and needless death of her son sent her on a lifetime campaign for pool safety. Yet it has been the small but meaningful contacts from her lost child that have brought her the most peace and healing.

My husband and I waited six years to have children. I was thirty-five when we had our first, our son, Nicholas. We were determined to do everything right in raising our child, so we read all the child care books we could find. I was almost obsessively cautious about anything that I thought could be hazardous to Nicholas's health and well-being. The thing that scared me the most was the pool in our own backyard. We knew that a fence was an absolute necessity to protect him. Before Nicholas started walking, we called a fencing company and had them install the tallest barricade they offered. Nicholas took his first steps the very next day.

Despite all the precautions, I continued to worry, especially after having a dream in which I saw Nicholas "asleep" in the pool.

It seemed that all my studying, worrying and loving paid off. Nicholas was growing up to be a great little boy. My son was an active child who had a tendency to turn over and dump out the contents of every toy box he laid eyes on. He must have thought the best toys were hidden at the bottom. At age two, he learned how to color and enjoyed being read stories. *Goodnight Moon* was his favorite book.

Since my husband and I both work, I made every effort to find Nicholas a safe daycare center. The provider I selected was a longtime friend of a friend who was just starting her business. Nicholas was her first charge. She and her two homeschooled daughters loved Nicholas like he was part of their family and they played with Nicholas constantly. It was everything I wanted in a care situation.

When the provider moved her home and daycare operation, I was extremely concerned about a spa in her new backyard. I have a dear friend whose daughter had drowned in a daycare spa twelve years earlier, so I was well aware of the danger it presented. Upon my insistence, the provider covered it, surrounded it with a locked fence and removed the stairs leading to its elevated perch. After that, I felt secure that there was no way Nicholas could get hurt.

As it turned out, the spa wasn't the problem.

On May 8, 1996, after I left Nicholas at the daycare center and arrived at work, I received a call from the daycare provider. I'll remember her words until the day I die. "Nicholas is alive. The paramedics are with him. He fell into a pool." She went on to explain that Nicholas had escaped her fenced backyard while the person watching the kids had to chase after a child who had dashed out through a gate. In the confusion, Nicholas scampered unseen through the open gate, wandered over to the neighbor's backyard and plunged into an unfenced swimming pool. Because of the thick, forest-like foliage and the distance between the homes, I hadn't even been aware there was a pool next door.

The rest of the day was a blur. My office manager drove me to the provider's home. I got there in time to witness the paramedics giving Nicholas CPR and then watch as he was airlifted to a children's hospital. My husband later joined me at the hospital.

The doctors performed numerous tests and determined that although Nicholas was breathing, he was essentially gone. He had been in the water too long. Late that evening, we decided to turn off the machines and let him go. I held him in my arms and gently rocked him back and forth, listening as his breathing grew softer and softer until it finally stopped at 10:00 P.M. He was two years, three months and nine days old.

When Nicholas fell into that pool, he had no chance to survive. Too young to swim and with no one around, he was doomed. Few people are aware of how dangerous back-yard swimming pools can be. Any unsecured pool is a hazard. Preventing a tragic accident of this nature is easy. All it takes is a locked fence.

As a way of coping with Nicholas's loss, I've devoted myself to working for upgraded pool fence regulations to help save other children from this terrible fate. I believe there should be a national law that all pools must be fenced. Such a law should have teeth, with strong enforcement and even stronger penalties for noncompliance.

I've joined an E-mail loop with other bereaved moms. This has been a tremendous comfort and has helped me to cope with my loss.

I also talk about Nicholas all the time. I answer honestly when people ask me how many children I have. I tell them I have an eighteen-month-old on earth and a two-year-old in heaven. When they ask what happened, I don't hesitate to tell them. Because of this, Nicholas's life and death have made a great impact in increasing awareness of the pool fence issue. In fact, one of the paramedics who attended to Nicholas at the scene, Paul Maxwell, joined the Safe Kids Coalition and now lobbies for rigid pool safety laws as well. He was named paramedic of the year in the state of California for his efforts.

There is nothing more precious than our children. We must protect them, because they can't protect themselves. I urge everyone I meet to work toward the creation and enforcement of pool protection laws in communities throughout the nation.

Nicholas's Contacts

I've had several vivid dreams about Nicholas that have shown me that he's with loved ones and is okay. In one, he was sitting with my grandfather who died many years ago. They were reading a book together and both appeared content. Then my son and grandfather looked up at me with expressions that convey to me that I shouldn't worry about them, that they are fine.

In addition, a close friend has shared with me a series of very odd dreams that she's had. In her early dreams, Nicholas appeared to be worried about his earth family and how we were coping without him. However, as time has passed, in my friend's dreams, Nicholas has grown less and less concerned about his family as he adapts to his spiritual existence.

I miss Nicholas very much. However, I believe that God is in control. He is the only one who knows the answers to all my questions. Someday, God will give me the answers and, on that day, I will have Nicholas in my arms again.

– Lynn Rosecrans

A strange dream, a name called out, a fleeting sound or vision—they may seem insignificant, but to mothers and fathers who have lost their precious children, such "minor" moments bring deep and long-lasting peace and healing. For it is in those moments that parents learn their children have gone to a better place where they are happy, safe and free.

Chapter Nine

Diary of a Child's Contacts

While some parents experience one or two brief contacts made by a child after death, others experience several. Still others, like Tamera Daniels, are blessed with lengthy and ongoing interactions with their departed children. This continuous contact has had such a profound impact on Tamera, and all surviving members of the Daniels family, that she chronicled them in her diary. Though all the parents' stories could not be shared in such detail, what follows is the story of Justin Daniels's life and Tamera's diary of his touching after death interactions with his family.

My son, Justin, was a baseball fanatic who loved everything about the game, from playing it himself, to being an enthusiastic fan, to collecting hundreds of cards. His favorite team was the Seattle Mariners. His dream was to play for them one day.

Justin was the oldest of our four children and took that responsibility without complaint, pitching in with his sister Kristle to help care for our two youngest daughters, Sierra and Kelsey. My fondest memories are of him playing with his sisters or reading to them. You could see in Justin's big, brown eyes how much he loved his sisters.

Though he could be mischievous at times, Justin was well-mannered and overall, simply a good kid.

On Sunday afternoon, March 23, 1997, Justin came into the kitchen and asked if he could meet his friend at school to play baseball. I said he could, but told him to be back by 4:30 P.M. Justin hopped on his bike and took off with his big, black, bat bag hanging on his back. I momentarily wondered if it was safe for him to carry such an awkward bag on his bicycle, but I dismissed the idea, thinking it the fear of an overprotective mother's mind.

Later in the afternoon, as I was making dinner, I heard emergency tones ring out from the police scanner we had in the house. I stopped what I was doing to listen to the machine that we kept for my husband, Pat, who is a fire rescue officer. "Aid 264, Medic 35....Car versus pedestrian." Startled, my thoughts immediately turned to Justin. I checked the clock to see if it was time for him to be coming home. It was. "Car versus pedestrian on bicycle" the radio crackled. In that moment, I felt certain it was Justin who had been hit by a car. I told my oldest daughter to stay home and watch her sisters, then I sprinted toward the door and ran down the street. My husband, who was also heading to the scene of the accident, pulled up alongside me in his car and tried to convince me to turn around and go home. I yelled, "No!" and jumped in his car to go with him. He didn't argue.

When we reached the scene, Pat shot out of the vehicle before I could even move and quickly knelt by a figure laying on the pavement. Just as we feared, it was our Justin.

Someone ran over and grabbed me, preventing me from joining my husband at my son's side. I turned my attention to the crowd and snapped "Which one of you hurt my boy?" A young woman was sobbing and being held very tightly by someone, so I knew it was she. There was no point in confronting her, because I could see that she was devastated by the accident.

I wanted so badly to go to Justin, but my husband kept yelling "No! Keep her there. Don't let her over here!" I calmed down enough to take in the scene. There was a white car parked nearby with a shattered windshield and busted out sunroof. Justin's bike was a few feet away, mangled beyond recognition. "We need airlift. Now!" Pat's authoritative voice rang out. I knew that meant Justin was severely injured. I begged everyone to please allow me to see my son before they packed him into the rescue helicopter. Pat finally came over and walked me back to him. Justin was lying at the end of someone's driveway, covered by a quilt. His eyes were only partially open and were very dark. His skin was a disquietingly odd color.

"I'm here," I assured my son. "I love you very much." His head turned toward me, but his eyes remained dark. I knew then that he was starting his journey to the next existence—but I refused to accept it.

A neighbor offered to drive me home to get my shoes. I had sprinted out of the house so fast I didn't stop to put shoes on. Gratefully, I accepted the ride. When we reached the house, I ran inside, gathered my shoes and extra clothes for both my husband and myself. Despite my gut feeling on the street about Justin's imminent passing, I now convinced myself that my husband and I would need extra clothes because we'd be at the hospital for days, possibly weeks, until our son was well enough to come home. Before leaving my house, I asked my neighbor to watch my daughters and she kindly took them home with her.

Back at the scene, Justin had been hoisted into an

ambulance and was on his way to a landing zone at the ele-
mentary school around the corner. I followed him there and
peeked inside the ambulance. The medics were performing
emergency CPR and it chilled my soul. I felt a pressure on my
chest as if it was me lying on the stretcher receiving CPR. I
wanted to trade places with my son so badly that I tried to get
inside the ambulance. Pat and another firefighter pulled me
away. "Do you realize what they're doing? They're doing
CPR!" I screamed. The firefighter claimed it was a routine
procedure because of the drugs used to paralyze a patient in
order to get the tubes in, but I knew that wasn't true. I had
been a fireman's wife too long to fall for that.

After the helicopter landed, Justin was loaded on and
the helicopter took off, my husband and I got in the car and
raced toward the hospital. Our route took us across a new
overpass in Redmond. In the distance, I could see the helicopter that carried Justin. My husband kept saying, "He'll be
okay, Tammi. He's a strong kid. He'll be okay." I wanted to
believe him, but everything inside me told me the opposite
would happen. I was torn up inside, one minute convincing
myself Justin would be okay, the next minute fearing the
worst. As we hit the 520 bridge into Seattle, the most inde-
scribable pain pierced my heart. It felt like a piece of it was
being torn from inside my chest. That was followed by an
overwhelming sense of emptiness. I started to cry. Pat held
my hand and whispered, "He'll be okay." Despite my husband's words of encouragement, I felt sure Justin wouldn't
be okay, but I couldn't bear to tell my husband. As the minutes passed, I went into full denial to keep myself from
falling apart, pretending that everything was going to work
out. Deep down, however, my mother's instinct told me my
boy was gone.

At the hospital, it wasn't long before the doctors

confirmed my feelings. "I'm very sorry to tell you, but your son passed away a few moments ago."

"No!" I screamed, lunging at the doctor as if it was her fault. Pat grabbed me and pulled me away. "Liar! Liar!" I accused. I was so emotionally overwrought, I turned on my own husband. "I'll never forgive you for not letting me hold my son!" The hurt look in his eyes knocked some sense back into me. I suddenly realized what I'd said and how it affected my husband. I've wished a thousand times I could take back those awful words.

Struggling to regain my composure, I attempted to apologize to the doctor but she was dubious about my ability to control myself. I gave up trying to convince her I wasn't crazed and instead begged her to let me see Justin. She told us we could see him later. Though the words seemed inadequate, I then apologized to my husband for lashing out at him. He told me that it was alright, that he understood. We hugged and cried for our boy.

As we waited at the hospital, I found myself too wound up to sit, so I paced the hallway instead. Finally, a social worker appeared and told us we could see Justin. We were warned that the tubes were still in his mouth and that it wasn't a pretty sight. We walked down a long corridor until she directed us toward a doorway. As we entered the room, I noticed it was cold and eerily quiet. I looked at my son. Justin was covered with a white sheet up to his shoulders. I tried to block the shocking images of injuries and medical equipment and instead enjoy this last moment, stroking his hair and holding his hand. Just as things seemed to become almost peaceful, my mother-in-law came in and promptly fainted. Thankfully, my father-in-law alertly caught her before she hit the floor. The emergency room personnel ushered her into another room to make sure she was okay.

Someone on the hospital staff came into the room and gave me a chair. I sat next to the gurney and leaned toward my son. "I love you, baby," I whispered into Justin's ear. "Go be with the angels. Mommy will miss you."

We left the room where Justin was and I immediately tried to find the doctor who had given us the bad news to apologize again, but it was too late; she was gone. Then I began calling and gathering the rest of the family. I knew we were going to donate Justin's organs, so anyone who wanted to see him to say goodbye had to do so then and there.

On the way home that evening, as we crossed the I-90 bridge, we saw a lunar eclipse, along with the Hale-Bopp comet. It was the first time I was able to see the comet after trying many nights during the previous week. Now, the celestial event seemed so insignificant.

At home, I walked through the house feeling lost and alone. I feared my husband would shut down and lock everyone out so I voiced this concern to him. I told him I needed him to be open about his emotions. Tragedies such as this have been known to tear apart solid, long-term relationships and I didn't want this to happen to us. He promised to work on being communicative with me.

When the girls came home from my neighbor's house, we took them into the living room and sat on the couch. I held the youngest ones, Kelsey and Sierra, while Pat sat beside me with Kristle. We told them that Justin was hurt really bad and that he had gone to be with the angels in heaven. Kristle, immediately understanding the gravity of the situation, cried out "No!" and began sobbing. Sierra also started to cry. Kelsey, the youngest, didn't quite understand what I had said, so she asked if the angels would fix Justin and send him back to us. I explained that Justin's body wouldn't work anymore, so his spirit went with the angels and he couldn't come back. Then we all cried together.

That evening, I hardly slept a wink. I got up a few times and went into Justin's room, hoping to find him there in his bed where he belonged. I sat in the living room for a long time trying to understand what happened and where we would go from here. *How can I help my husband and daughters get through this? How will I get through this?* I watched it get lighter and lighter outside as the terrible night melted into morning. When we had left the hospital, I asked our family or friends not to come over, instead wanting to be left alone. But in the morning, I begged Pat, "Please call someone, anyone. It's too quiet and I need people around." Our home was soon overflowing with family and friends and stayed that way for a week. Being surrounded by loved ones helped us get through those toughest, darkest days at the beginning.

The years have sped by, but we still miss Justin every single minute of every day. Sometimes I wonder how we've survived without him. How did we just go on with our lives? Since we have no choice, we will continue to live until it's time for all of us to be together again.

We've been fortunate to have experienced a great number of contacts with Justin since his passing. Because of the sudden nature of the accident, he no doubt simply wasn't ready to go and for that reason, he seems still closely bonded to his family on earth. I hope that by sharing with others Justin's contacts, they will find comfort in the knowledge that life does not end with death, but continues on.

Justin's Contacts

March 24, 1997

Kristle, who is still in shock only a day after her brother's death, was too upset to sleep in her own bed so she asked if she could sleep on the couch. Ten minutes after we said good night, she came running into our room, crying and looking frightened. "I heard him. I heard Justin! He whispered in my ear!" she exclaimed. I told her that she shouldn't be afraid of her brother and I asked what he said.

"He told me that he loves me," Kristle answered.

I assured Kristle that her brother was not trying to frighten her. He knew she would only believe he was okay if she heard it directly from him.

This was our first visit from Justin and I hope it won't be our last.

April 24, 1997

It was a nice day today and Kelsey and I spent it outside. She was playing on her swing, while I sat on the front porch reading. Kelsey started asking questions about Justin and I answered them the best that I could. Then she asked, "Mommy, why was Justin wearing a blue nightgown when he came to see me?" I asked her when he came to see her and she said, "All the time. At night, when I'm in bed." I asked her if he came into her room and she answered, "No, he was in my window and he was wearing a blue nightgown." Though strange, for some reason, Kelsey's description of her brother sounded vaguely familiar. After a moment, I thought of something that I had seen in the medical examiners report and fished it out again. We never discussed the contents of this report with any of Justin's sisters because we felt they were too young to understand. Plus, I hadn't been able to get completely through the report myself. Reading it through now, I saw a notation that he was wearing a blue hospital gown. The last time Kelsey saw Justin, he was wearing blue jeans and a T-shirt. He never wore nightgowns of any kind. That made me believe Justin must have visited his baby sister.

May 8, 1997

Kelsey and I were in the living room, spending time together. She started asking more questions about Justin, so I picked her up, placed her on my lap and tried to answer them as simply and honestly as I could. I asked her if Justin had visited her again. She said he comes to her room often at night. I asked her if he ever touched her or if she could she touch him. She answered that she couldn't touch him, because when she tried, her hand went right through him. As she explained this, she motioned with her hand to demonstrate how she had tried to touch her brother. I began to wonder if what is often said of young children is true—that they are more open to this type of paranormal activity. Is Justin visiting his sister? I really hope so.

May 14, 1997

I was sitting on the front porch today when I heard someone call out, "Mom." I heard it twice. Kristle and Sierra were in school and Kelsey was in the living room engrossed in a television program. I went inside to check on Kelsey, but she assured me she hadn't called for me. I went back outside and heard it again: "Mom." I'm not sure I can accept what I want to believe about this. I want to believe it was Justin who called for me.

May 17, 1997

Today, I received a picture in the mail from Kyla, my six-year-old niece. It was a drawing of Justin. In the drawing, Justin is wearing a dark blue shirt and a small silver necklace. Kyla also drew, very lightly, some wings on Justin. This picture is extraordinary because Kyla didn't attend Justin's memorial service yet in her drawing Justin is wearing exactly what he had on that day: a dark blue Mariner's shirt, jeans and his silver St. Christopher medal around his neck. I talked to Kyla's mother and learned that no family members who had attended Justin's service had told Kyla about it. I wonder if Justin visits his little cousin in dreams or if she actually sees him. I hope she sees him, because it helps me believe that someday I'll see him as well.

May 18, 1997
Justin's Aunt Kelly called me today. She had a dream about Justin and wanted to tell me about it. This is a description of Kelly's dream in her words:

"I was outside, surrounded by all the kids. They were laughing and playing. It was a beautiful, sunny day—blue sky, green grass, blue water and a wooden dock. As I was watching the kids, I saw Justin running and laughing with them. I did a double-take, calling out, 'Justin, is that really you? Are you really here?' He looked at me, smiled and said, 'It's me, Aunt Kelly. I'm really here. I will always be here.'"

Kelly said over and over how vivid her dream was and how different it was from any other dream she has ever had. She also said that she could actually feel Justin when she touched him. I believe Justin visited his aunt while she was asleep.

December, 1997
During this holiday season, Justin sent us many signs that he is most definitely with us. On two separate occasions, two different televisions turned off. The outside lights were turned on in the middle of the night. We've heard the footsteps of someone walking around in his room and have had strange sounds come from our computer.

I have been asking Justin, every night since his death, for a specific sign to let me know he is okay. I want something personal, just to me—a sign that will help me comfort other family members and friends.

More than a year ago, in April 1996, I bought a watch with an angel on its face. I wear it whenever I leave the house. I was out doing some grocery shopping for Christmas, checked the time and noticed that the second hand wasn't moving. This didn't make sense to me, because I had replaced the battery a few weeks before. I didn't really give it much more thought though. I just told myself I would have to replace the watch's battery again the next time I had a chance. When I got home, I took the watch off in the garage in order to help my husband with the Christmas tree. After dinner, my husband went to the fire station for an all night shift. I got the kids settled in bed, then relaxed in front of the television while preparing some presents. After the news, I searched the channels for something interesting and came upon a program about spirits. A guest on the show stated that spirits are pure energy and can affect anything with an energy source, including a watch. Upon hearing this, I immediately went out to the garage and located my watch. When I looked at it, I saw that both hands had now stopped. My son's death certificate popped into my head. I took the watch inside, found the death certificate and almost fainted. Justin was pronounced dead by the Emergency Room doctor at 17:59. My watch was stopped at exactly 5:59! I began to cry. As I sat on my couch holding the watch, I spoke through my tears to Justin. "Is this from you? Is this for me?"

In my heart, I know that Justin is okay and that this was a sign from him. When I mentioned the stopped watch the next day to my husband, he told me to never install a new battery in the watch. He said the odds of my watch stopping at that exact time are so phenomenal that we have to believe it's a message from Justin. Instead, we put it away for safe keeping. He bought me a new angel watch for Christmas—this one has a little boy angel on the face.

January 1998

My parents sold their house and bought a motor home which they have temporarily set up on my property. They plan to begin traveling around the country when the warm weather of spring arrives.

February 14, 1998

My friend, Lora, and her young daughter, Brittney, came over to spend the weekend with us. Lora is having problems with her older daughter, who had been very close to Justin. Apparently, Lora's older daughter isn't handling Justin's death very well.

After all of the kids were in bed, Lora and I were sitting in my living room talking about her older daughter and some of what has been going on since Justin passed. Lora wasn't sure how to help the girl deal with her grief. As she was talking, she suddenly stopped in mid-sentence and turned very quickly to look back over her shoulder. She did a double-take. When she turned back towards me, she was absolutely ashen and couldn't catch her breath. I was afraid she was having an attack of some kind. I asked her several times what was wrong. She finally composed herself and explained that as we were talking, she sensed that someone was standing behind her. When she turned the first time, there was a figure standing in the hallway. When she looked back the second time, the figure had vanished. She said she was sure it was Justin. I wasn't surprised. I'm certain that she saw my son. Maybe he wanted to let her know that he was there to comfort her and was trying to let us know that Lora's older daughter would be okay.

April 1, 1998

We found out on April 1 that my father has terminal lung cancer. The past week has been a blur of doctors, hospitals and treatments. Sadly, my parents will not get to travel as they had planned.

April 10, 1998

With my dad's health problems weighing heavily on my mind, today was depressing all the way around. This morning, my mom and dad were at the hospital, my two older daughters were at school, Lora picked up Kelsey to play with Brittney and my husband was at work. I was left alone and began feeling sorry for myself. I sat on my front porch, thinking about Justin and my dad. I realized that the last three springs have brought tragedy and sadness to our lives. In April 1996, our home and everything inside was destroyed by fire. In March 1997, Justin was killed in an auto accident. And now, in 1998, my robust, healthy, fifty-six-year-old father has been diagnosed with deadly cancer.

To deal with it all, I decided to talk to Justin. I asked him if he could help me be strong. "I could sure use one of your hugs right now!" I said. I wanted him to let me know for absolute certain that he was with us. To do so, I requested something specific—a rainbow. And not just any rainbow, but a special one that was as close as he could place it. Though it was a little cloudy, all-in-all it was a nice morning for Washington. Unfortunately, there were no rainbows in sight.

Later in the day, Lora came by with her daughters to return Kelsey home. A short while after they arrived, the weather changed dramatically. Lightning flashed, thunder shook the house and it began pouring rain. By this time, with the scary storm and visitors diverting my attention, I'd completely forgotten about my earlier request of my son.

Suddenly, Kelsey hollered, "Mommy, Mommy! Look! A rainbow in the lake!"

I peered out through the French doors to the lake that lies behind our property and couldn't believe what I saw: a wondrous rainbow that started smack in the middle of the water! The colors were so bright it was as if you could reach out and touch them. I ran to my parents' motor home to see if they returned from the hospital. They had. I told them that I'd asked Justin for this particular rainbow. My father and I stood together at the back door and watched in awe as the giant rainbow became brighter, then slowly faded away.

I will never forget the feeling of peace that I had being there with my dad. I know that this was a sign from Justin to let us know that he was watching over us through this very difficult time.

November 4, 1998
My father has been fighting terminal lung cancer for the last eight months. The doctors told us a few days ago that his time is coming to an end. Dad had made me promise that I wouldn't let him die in the hospital, so we brought him home. Pat and I set up our bedroom with a special bed and everything else Dad needs.

I woke up this morning feeling as though something was different. The atmosphere inside the house was odd. It's very difficult to put this into words; I just knew that something was going to happen. I spent most of the day sitting with my father. Later in the afternoon, we knew he was getting worse, so we alerted friends and the rest of the family and asked them to come over. We also called a hospice nurse to assist us. Although he was unconscious, dad seemed so agitated that we thought he was in great distress. The nurse gave him some medication to calm his nerves and dull the pain. Suddenly, he opened his eyes and tried to sit up. He stretched out his arms as if to reach for someone. My mother thought he was reaching for her, but he pushed her away and continued reaching behind her. Then he slumped back onto his pillow and was gone.

A little while later, I called my sister-in-law to tell her that Dad had passed away. She asked me what time he died. I told her he passed away at 8:15 P.M. She told me that at that precise time, she had been in her kitchen and had a vision of Justin with his arms outstretched calling for my father. "Grampa, it's time. You can come with me now," Justin had said.

Although it's hard for some people to believe in such things, it's clear to me that Dad was reaching out for Justin. I am very comforted to know that they are together now, and that I will be with them someday.

– Tamera Daniels

Like the other parents who shared their stories, Tamera Daniels has grieved terribly for the son she lost. However, she's also found beauty and happiness in life, in large part due to her son's ongoing messages of love.

Epilogue

When Donna Theisen first approached me to ask me to help her write this book, I was skeptical. It's not that I'm close-minded about the supernatural. I actually loved the idea and truly believe in after death contacts. After all, they appear in the Bible. Plus, my old world Italian family has been telling me stories about such phenomena my entire life. The problem was that most of the accounts Donna initially sent appeared to be regular dreams and routine coincidences. Obviously, an emotionally overwrought, grieving parent desperately searching for signs that his or her child is still around, will find coincidences at every turn.

Donna herself fell into this category. She saw her son Michael in butterflies, eagles, clocks, ringing phones, mosquitoes, gnats, anything and everything. I teased her that if the sun rose in the morning, she'd see it as a message from Michael. In typical fashion, she responded "It would be!"

As I poured myself into the actual writing of the book, more and more stories arrived recounting events that went far beyond "routine coincidences." Even the dreams had resplendent qualities about them that made it obvious from my perspective that something truly phenomenal was happening between these parents and their lost children.

Now that I was convinced, I was still left with the dilemma of what to do about the smaller, less dramatic contacts other parents were telling me about. It seemed somewhat cruel to exclude people from the book just because their child's spirit didn't seem as creative as another's or because their child's energy and ability to break the divide between life and death wasn't as strong or developed as someone else's offspring. In contrast, as an author, I didn't want to water down the book with "weaker" stories.

As I was struggling with this, a series of events happened that provided the answer. First, I began receiving E-mails from Donna claiming that her son Michael was appearing to "virtual friends" she had met on the Internet. I found this to be highly questionable. Why would Michael contact people across the country that Donna hardly knew? It didn't seem logical—that is, if logic plays any part in this kind of thing to begin with. On the other hand, I was made aware of similar incidences through stories told to me by a number of grieving parents. Often, when two grieving mothers who meet on the Internet or through a support group form a special bond and share their stories, they soon begin having dreams and visions of their departed children being together. The theory is, I guess, that the "Angel Children" remain so involved in their mother's lives that they are aware of these new friendships and form their own similar bonds in the afterlife. Though such an idea may be hard to swallow for some, stories of intertwined contacts have been repeated to me so often that I have come to believe that the truth of this idea must be considered a possibility.

Following along this path, Donna's son, Michael, could be viewed as a special case in that according to Donna, he was the force pushing her to write this book. So again, if one wants to adhere to some degree of "after death logic," it wouldn't be out of the ordinary for Michael to involve himself across the board in the process of gathering stories for the project.

Personally, I didn't want or expect to have any contacts. Fortunately, I haven't lost a child and I was initially terrified that being involved in such an effort would somehow doom my young son. Suffice it to say, I was not in anyway looking for contacts and therefore was not seeing coincidences at every turn. In fact, if anything, my attitude was, *All you kids just leave me alone and let me write the book. If you try to make contact, you're just going to scare me out of my skin and interfere with my work!*

It seems that Donna's Michael wasn't listening. The week of Valentine's Day, 2000, I saw an advertising flyer sitting on the island counter in my kitchen. It featured a sale on "Krinkle Dresses" at one of my favorite outlet stores. The flyer was all by itself, prominently displayed. I figured my wife was trying to drop a not-so-subtle hint about what she wanted for Valentine's Day. However, I knew it wasn't her style to leave an advertisement lying about like that. Plus, she wouldn't be caught dead in such a closeout bargain store and would be less than overwhelmed by a present from such a place. Further, she had long since stopped wearing clothes I bought her because our tastes are so different. I always bought her items like frilly party outfits in bright colors, while she prefers a more professional look and subdued tones.

The ad sat on the counter for a few days, then vanished. As Valentine's Day rapidly approached, like most men, I began to panic over what to get. I remembered the flyer and boldly asked if she was trying to give me a hint. She responded that if she wanted something, she'd simply tell me. "I wouldn't just leave out an ad. That's silly." Not only that, she denied having put the flyer there and claimed to have not even seen it. "I don't know what you are talking about. I wouldn't want something from that place anyway. I toss those flyers in the trash, ASAP." Although expected, her reaction was strange to me because the flyer was in the exact spot where she puts her papers everyday when she comes home from work and it remained there for at least two days. I couldn't understand how she'd not even seen it.

I decided to let it go and stopped thinking about it. However, as I was running errands the next day, I found myself stopping at that outlet store. Once inside, I thought of the mysterious "Krinkle Dress" ad and decided to take a look. There was a rack full of the dresses. They came in a series of bright, dramatic colors with vivid designs and were sewn from flowing, "krinkly" stretch material. I thought they looked nice, but were definitely not my wife's style.

Even so, I absentmindedly strummed through the racks. I came across a gray number dotted with beautiful butterflies, including many with prominent yellow wings. It was the only one of its kind among the fifty or so dresses available. I immediately thought of Donna Theisen and her contact with Michael when he came in the form of a butterfly. I knew the butterfly meant so much to her. "Hmmmm," I wondered aloud, "I bet Donna would like this. I wonder if I should get it for her?"

Though I had worked on another book with Donna, I never thought to buy her a gift, especially not an article of clothing like a dress! It seemed somewhat inappropriate. So, I dashed the thought and went about my business in the store. Yet for some reason, I kept being drawn back to the "Krinkle Dress" rack. I searched for any others with the butterfly design, maybe a brighter color than gray, but that seemed to be the only one. "What the heck," I thought, snatching it up. "Donna will like it. She'll probably see it as some kind of sign."

When I arrived home, I was still curious about the mystery ad. The trash recycle pick-up date wasn't until the following day, so I knew it had to still be around the house somewhere. I searched the recycling bin, the kitchen counter where it first appeared, the regular trash and everywhere else and couldn't find that flyer.

It finally dawned on me that this was all way too weird and way out of character for me to be so generous as to buy Donna Theisen a dress. It couldn't have been some kind of bizarre coincidence either. There was simply far too elaborate a string of factors that led me to that particular garment. I came to the conclusion that mischievous Michael must have wanted to give his mother that specific gift for Valentine's Day. He placed the ad in my kitchen so I'd think it was from my wife and I'd go to the store and find it. That explains why my wife never saw it and why it disappeared. Goosebumps covered my skeptical hide more than once as I contemplated this.

"Hey, Michael," I said. "Sorry I was so dense. I'll pack up the dress and mail it to your mom on the double."

Of course, the message behind this incident goes beyond a man wanting to give his grieving mother a memorable Valentine's Day gift. I believe Donna's son was sending me the answer I needed regarding the "lesser" stories in this book. Despite my inherent preference for high octane, Hollywood style, dramatic visions and contacts, I couldn't overlook the power behind the small, seemingly minor ones. The misplaced objects, key chain lights, funny telephone rings, stopped clocks, oddly behaving animals and, most of all, the butterflies, are just as real as the more theatrical contacts involving children who appear in full-bodied form, hug their parents or siblings, speak to them, then vanish into the mist.

I received Michael's message loud and clear. With his help, *Childlight* was written. My hope is that it will comfort his mother and her new friends and enable their children to "live forever" and never be forgotten. Plus, hopefully, it will give assurance and hope to millions of other parents who have lost children and desperately need to believe that their beloved children are still with us, healed and happy, existing on another, far more joyful plane.

Appendix A

Getting Help

The purpose of *Childlight* is to share grieving parents' stories in an effort to provide consolation and bring hope to others dealing with losses of their own. As a companion to the stories told in this book, a listing of resources, organizations, Web sites and government agencies is provided below. Groups designed to support and aid the bereaved as well as to provide information about such topics as suicide and organ donation are included in the following categories: Bereaved Parents, Drug/Alcohol Addiction, Grief Support, Illnesses, Murder Victims, Organ Donation, Pregnancy/Infant Loss and Suicide.

BEREAVED PARENTS

This section includes organizations and resources designed specifically for bereaved parents, so they can unite with others who have been through similar tragedies and receive comfort and support.

Alive Alone

http://www.alivealone.org

E-mail: KayBevington@alivealone.org

11115 Dull Robinson Road

Van Wert, Ohio 45891

Founded by Kay and Rodney Bevington after the loss of their only daughter, Rhonda, Alive Alone is a non-profit, educational and charitable organization created specifically to benefit bereaved parents whose child or children are deceased. It provides a self-help network and publications to promote communication and healing and to assist parents in resolving grief along with a means to reinvest their lives for a positive future. To receive the newsletter, visit their Web site or contact the Bevingtons via their mailing address or E-mail.

Bereaved Parents USA

http://www.bereavedparentsusa.org

E-mail: jgoodrch@megsinet.net

P.O. Box 95

Park Forest, Illinois 60466

Telephone: (630) 971-3490

Fax: (708) 748-9184

Bereaved Parents USA is a nationwide organization that aids and supports grieving parents and their families. Any bereaved parent, grandparent or sibling is eligible to become a member. Members are free to attend monthly meetings of one of the many chapters throughout the United States as often and for as long as they need to. There are no dues charged to belong to the organization, however tax-deductible, voluntary donations are welcome and may be made to the parent organization or an individual chapter. The organization is non-denominational, however members are free to state their beliefs and explain how religion has played a role in their lives. As of January 2001, there were chapters in eighteen U.S. states.

The Compassionate Friends

http://www.compassionatefriends.org

E-mail: nationaloffice@compassionatefriends.org

P.O. Box 3696

Oak Brook, Illinois 60522-3696

Telephone: (630) 990-0010

Fax: (630) 990-0246

The mission of The Compassionate Friends, a non-profit, self-help support organization, is to provide grief support to families after the loss of a child through its resources, literature, surveys and meetings at chapters located in all fifty states, Canada and throughout the world. There is no religious affiliation and no membership fees or dues. All bereaved family members are welcome.

Motivated On-line Moms (M.O.M.s)

http://hometown.aol.com/suzique47

Many of the stories presented in this book came from members of Motivated On-line Moms (M.O.M.s), a growing organization of grieving mothers who have bonded together on the Internet through a vibrant E-mail loop to give each other comfort and support. The grassroots M.O.M.s organization has quickly expanded from being an Internet E-pen pals loop to a group that holds meetings and retreats in various cities. The members of M.O.M.s also make quilts for terminally ill children and provide assistance to needy families. Once a year, the members of this positive change group meet in person and share their stories.

For more information, you can contact via E-mail M.O.M.s founder Bonnie Blankenship at Bjm797@aol.com or Donna Theisen at DeLaine089@aol.com.

My Parents Are Survivors
http://www.moms-dads.com
P.O. Box 418
Mango, Florida 33550-0418
This Internet support group for parents who have lost a child
holds on-line chats and has local chapters throughout the
country. Started in 1997 to help mothers set up memorials on
the Web for the children they lost, the site rapidly expanded
to meet the needs of its users to include fathers, grandparents and siblings.

Pen-Parents, Inc.
http://www.penparents.org
E-mail: penparents@penparents.org
P.O. Box 8738
Reno, Nevada 89507-8738
Telephone: (702) 826-7332
Fax: (702) 829-0866
Founded by a bereaved parent looking for a "pen-pal" network
to help those who don't feel comfortable with traditional sup-
port group meetings, Pen-Parents, Inc. is a non-profit organi-
zation that networks grieving parents to each other so they can
find consolation and support.

DRUG/ALCOHOL ADDICTION
This section contains information for government agencies
that deal specifically with alcohol and drug abuse.

National Institute on Alcohol Abuse and Alcoholism
http://www.niaaa.nih.gov
6000 Executive Boulevard - Willco Building
Bethesda, Maryland 20892-7003
This federal organization supports and conducts biomedical

and behavioral research on the causes, treatment and prevention of alcoholism and alcohol-related problems. The
organization provides statistics and data on alcohol abuse to
the public in its various publications, including an informa-
tive booklet designed specifically for parents.

National Institute on Drug Abuse

http://www.nida.nih.gov
6001 Executive Boulevard
Bethesda, Maryland 20892-9561
Telephone: (301) 443-1124
Established in 1974, NIDA funds scientific research on drug
abuse and addiction in an effort to improve prevention and
treatment. NIDA provides the latest information to the public through their Web site and various publications.

GRIEF SUPPORT

This section has Web sites and resources that provide support
and comfort to anyone grieving for a lost loved one, whether
he or she is a bereaved parent, friend, sibling or other family
member.

Center for Grief

http://griefloss.org
E-mail: cg@griefloss.org
Hamline Park Plaza, Suite 202
570 Asbury Street
Saint Paul, Minnesota 55104
Telephone: (651) 641-0177
Fax: (651) 641-8635
If you are a resident of Minnesota, you can take advantage of
this non-profit organization offering help and hope for those
who have experienced a significant loss in their lives. The

Center for Grief aims to improve the quality of care for grieving individuals and families through therapy, support groups and training for professionals and volunteers.

Centering Corporation
http://www.centering.org
E-mail: centering@centering.org
Telephone: (402) 553-1200
A non-profit organization, the Centering Corporation acts as a grief support resource center, offering books, videos, cards, dolls and other products for those affected by a loved one's death. The catalog of their products, which are geared for adults, children, parents, spouses, grandparents, siblings and friends, is available at their Web site or, for assistance, contact them directly via E-mail or telephone.

Death & Dying
http://www.death-dying.org
Launched in July 1997, the mission of Death & Dying is to offer a safe haven to those who have lost a loved one, are anticipating the loss of a loved one or who are facing their own death in the near future. Death & Dying provides comfort, support and education on issues surrounding death through its services including on-line chats, message boards, planners, articles, newsletters and information and facts on terminal illness and health issues.

GriefNet
http://rivendell.org
E-mail: cendra@griefnet.org
A non-profit corporation overseen by Cendra Lynn, clinical grief psychologist and death educator, GriefNet is an Internet community that deals with grief, death and major loss.

Through E-mail support groups, two Web sites, bulletin boards, a library and bookstore, GriefNet provides help to people working through grief and loss issues. Their companion site, KIDSAID (www.kidsaid.com), provides a safe environment for kids and their parents to get information and ask questions.

Grief Recovery On-line
http://www.groww.com
Grief Recovery On-line (GROWW) is a haven for the bereaved hosted by the bereaved. A place where peer groups meet in an on-line chat room environment, GROWW helps members permit themselves to grieve, understand the process of grieving, be open about their pain and receive comfort, strength and support from other members.

Journey of Hearts
http://www.journeyofhearts.org
The collaborative effort of physicians, colleagues, friends and on-line visitors, this Web site is for anyone who has ever experienced loss. It offers resources and support to help those working through the grief process. The Alliance of Healing Hearts Web-ring, part of Journey of Hearts, is a group of individuals united by the common bond of loss, who help each other survive and overcome their losses by sharing their stories and offering one another support.

Support-Group.com
http://www.support-group.com
This Web site allows people with a variety of health, personal and relationship problems or issues—including bereavement —to share their experiences through bulletin boards and on-line chats. The site also provides links to support-related information on the Internet.

ILLNESSES

Information, support and referral services are available through the following Web sites along with resources geared specifically toward family members and individuals wishing to learn more about the life-threatening illnesses that have affected their or their loved ones' lives. For information on Sudden Infant Death Syndrome (SIDS), refer to the section titled Pregnancy/Infant Loss.

American Cancer Society
http://www.cancer.org
Toll-free telephone: (800) ACS-2345
A nationwide, community-based voluntary health organization, the American Cancer Society is dedicated to eliminating cancer as a major health problem by preventing it, saving lives and diminishing suffering through research, education, advocacy and service. A variety of service and rehabilitation programs are available to patients and their families.

Families of Spinal Muscular Atrophy
http://www.fsma.org
P.O. Box 196
Libertyville, IL 60048-0196
Toll-free telephone: (800) 886-1762
Telephone: (847) 367-7620
Fax: (847) 367-7623
Families of Spinal Muscular Atrophy (SMA) was founded in 1984 for the purpose of raising funds to research the causes of SMA and to find a cure. Since then, this all-volunteer, non-profit organization has raised eight million dollars for SMA research. In addition to their efforts to eradicate Spinal

Muscular Atrophy, this organization works to educate the public and professional community about SMA and helps families cope with this illness through informational programs and support, on-line message boards and local chapters throughout the United States and Canada.

The Leukemia and Lymphoma Society
http://www.leukemia.org
Email: infocenter@leukemia-lymphoma.org
1311 Mamaroneck Avenue
White Plains, New York 10605
Telephone: (914) 949-5213
Fax: (914) 949-6691
This group has dedicated itself to finding a cure for leukemia, lymphoma, Hodgkin's disease and myeloma—all cancers of the blood—and to improve the quality of life for patients and their families through research, patient services, advocacy, revenue generation and raising public awareness.

National Childhood Cancer Foundation
http://www.nccf.org
440 East Huntington Drive
P.O. Box 60012
Arcadia, California 91066-6012
Toll-free telephone: (800) 458-NCCF
Fax: (626) 447-6359
The foundation supports a network of childhood cancer treatment and research institutions throughout North America where state-of-the-art laboratory research is conducted and first-class care is given to infants, children and teens with cancer. Information about these centers is available on their Web site.

The National Children's Cancer Society
http://www.children-cancer.com
1015 Locust, Suite 600
St. Louis, Missouri 63101
Toll-free telephone: (800) 532-6459
This non-profit organization is dedicated to providing financial support for expenses related to treatment to families who have children battling cancer. Working with more than 200 pediatric oncology hospitals and cancer centers to identify families in financial need, the society assists children in the United States from birth to age eighteen. Since its inception in 1987, the society has distributed in excess of $21,000,000 in direct financial assistance to more than 7,000 cancer-stricken children and their families.

National Down Syndrome Society
http://www.ndss.org
666 Broadway
New York, New York 10012
Toll-free telephone: (800) 221-4602
Telephone: (212) 460-9330
Fax: (212) 979-2873
The NDS Society was formed in 1979 to help people with Down Syndrome and their families. This non-profit organization is the largest non-governmental supporter of Down Syndrome research in the United States. Affiliate programs supported by the society include local groups for parent training, educational outreach and family support. The NDSS Web site acts as a comprehensive on-line information resource on Down Syndrome.

The Neuroblastoma Children's Cancer Society

http://www.granitewebworks.com/nccs.htm
P.O. Box 957672
Hoffman Estates, Illinois 60195
Toll-free telephone: (800) 532-5162
Fax: (847) 490-0705
This group, consisting mainly of volunteers, acts as an advocate for children and their families and is dedicated to providing support. The primary focus is to raise funds to assist research in neuroblastoma cancer until a cure is found. Their Web site answers common questions about the disease, offers a support chat room and hosts a "Wall of Fame" where information and photographs of children suffering from Neuroblastoma are posted.

MURDER VICTIMS

This section includes resources and Web sites with information and support for parents, friends and families of murder victims.

Murder Victims' Families for Reconciliation

http://www.mvfr.org
2161 Massachusetts Avenue
Cambridge, Massachusetts 02140
Telephone: (617) 868-0007
Fax: (617) 354-2832
An anti-capital punishment group comprised of the parents and siblings of murder victims, Murder Victims' Families for Reconciliation (MVFR) works to end the isolation of survivors of homicide victims and reinforce and support the notion

that it is okay to not want the murderer killed by the state. In addition to public education, policy reform, victim support and speaking tours, MVFR is holding the First National Gathering of Murder Victims' Family Members Who Oppose the Death Penalty in Boston, Massachusetts, May 31, 2001.

Office for Victims of Crime
http://www.ojp.usdoj.gov/ovc
E-mail: askovc@ojp.usdoj.gov
Department of Justice / Office for Victims of Crime
810 Seventh Street N.W.
Washington, D.C. 20531
Toll-free telephone: (800) 627-6872
Telephone: (202) 307-5983
Under the U.S. Department of Justice, the Office for Victims of Crime (OVC) was established by the 1984 Victims of Crime Act to oversee diverse programs that benefit victims of crime. OVC provides substantial funding to state victim assistance and compensation programs and supports training designed to educate criminal justice and allied professionals. Their Web site provides resource links, information and facts on crime in the United States, links to resources for victims and training information for professionals.

Parents of Murdered Children
http://www.pomc.com
E-mail: NatlPOMC@aol.com
100 East Eighth Street, Suite B-41
Cincinnati, Ohio 45202
Toll-free telephone: (888) 818-POMC
Telephone: (513) 721-5683
Fax: (513) 345-4489

The only national helping organization specifically for survivors of homicide victims, Parents of Murdered Children (POMC) also provides follow-up family services support after a murder of a loved one through their national headquarters and local chapters. POMC also provides advocacy to families and training to professionals in fields such as law enforcement, criminal justice, medicine, education, religion and the media. POMC also has a "traveling wall" that lists names of children that have fallen victim to murder (Brian Hotchkiss from chapter 5 is on Panel 7.) For a small donation, parents can add their child's name, biographical information and a photograph. The wall travels to local chapters around the country to raise awareness of child homicide.

ORGAN DONATION

For information on becoming an organ donor, how organ donation works and other issues regarding organ donation, please refer to the following Web sites and organizations.

Legacy Organ and Tissue Donor Registry of the Louisiana Organ Procurement Agency
http://www.lopa.org
3501 North Causeway Boulevard, Suite 940
Metairie, Louisiana 70002-3626
Toll-free telephone: (800) 521-GIVE
Telephone: (504) 837-3355
Tax: (504) 837-3587
The Louisiana Organ Procurement Agency (LOPA) is a nonprofit organ and tissue recovery agency that aims to enhance and promote the recovery of organs and tissues for transplant patients and help the community by providing support services which enhance the donation process. If you would

like more information or to join the registry and become a donor in memory of Justin Harrison (see chapter 2) or another individual, please visit their Web site or call their toll-free telephone number.

United Network for Organ Sharing
http://www.unos.org
The United Network for Organ Sharing, or UNOS, is a private, non-profit organization that administers the National Organ Procurement and Transplantation Network, under contract with the U.S. Department of Health and Human Services. Through their Organ Center, UNOS manages the national transplant waiting list, matching donors to recipients.

PREGNANCY/INFANT LOSS
The following resources provide support and information for mothers and fathers who have experienced the loss of a pregnancy or a newborn child.

American SIDS Institute
http://www.sids.org
2480 Windy Hill Road, Suite 380
Marietta, Georgia 30067
Toll-free telephone: (800) 232-SIDS
Telephone: (770) 612-1030
Founded in 1983, the American SIDS Institute, a national, non-profit health care organization, is dedicated to the prevention of sudden infant death syndrome and the promotion of infant health through an aggressive, comprehensive national program of research, clinical services, education and family support.

CareNotes Publications
Telephone: (800) 325-2511
Provides literature on infant loss.

M.E.N.D. (Mommies Enduring Neonatal Death)
http://www.mend.org
E-mail: rebekah@mend.org
P.O. Box 1007
Coppell, Texas 75019
Toll-free telephone: (888) 695-MEND
This non-profit, Christian organization provides support for those who have lost a child to miscarriage, stillbirth or early infant death by allowing them to share their experiences with others suffering similar losses through support groups. Information and guidance are also offered through the Web site and a bi-monthly newsletter.

M.I.S.S.
http://www.misschildren.org
E-mail: joanne@misschildren.org
P.O. Box 5333
Peoria, Arizona 85385-5333
A non-profit, volunteer organization, M.I.S.S. provides emergency support to parents after the death of their baby, stillbirth, neonatal death, premature birth, congenital anomalies, SIDS or any child's death. The organization also works to raise public awareness to decrease infant mortality, supports medical research committed to the same cause, offers workshops and seminars on grief and therapy and provides information on pre- and post-natal care. Please visit their Web site or for information, contact the founder, Joanne Cacciatore, via E-mail.

National Sudden Infant Death Syndrome Resources Center (NSRC)
http://www.circsol.com/sids/
E-mail: sids@circsol.com
2070 Chain Bridge Road, Suite 450
Vienna, VA 22182
Telephone: (703) 821-8955
Fax: (703) 821-2098
NSRC provides information and services on SIDS and related topics in an effort to promote understanding of SIDS and to provide comfort to those affected by this illness. NSRC's products and services include publications (e.g. *What is SIDS?*, *Sudden Infant Death Syndrome: Facts You Should Know*) and referral services. For additional information, please check their Web site or contact them via E-mail, fax or the mailing address listed above.

SHARE – Pregnancy and Infant Loss Support
National Share Office
http://www.nationalshareoffice.com
St. Joseph Health Center
300 First Capitol Drive
St. Charles, Missouri 63301-2893
Toll-free telephone: (800) 821-6819
Telephone: (636) 947-6164
Fax: (636) 947-7486
SHARE is a non-profit group that provides support and guidance to parents after the loss of a pregnancy or infant through literature, bi-monthly newsletters, phone calls and support meetings.

SIDS Alliance
http://www.sidsalliance.org
E-mail: sidshq@charm.net
1314 Bedford Avenue, Suite 210
Baltimore, Maryland 21208
Telephone: (410) 653-8226
Fax: (410) 653-8709
Formed through the merger of national and regional SIDS groups, the SIDS Alliance was established in 1987 in an effort to unite parents and friend of SIDS victims with medical, business and civic groups concerned about the health of America's babies. The goal is to increase public awareness, strengthen ongoing efforts to expand scientific and research programs, increase services for families and provide advocacy.

Sudden Infant Death Syndrome Network, Inc.
http://www.sidsnet@sids-network.org
E-mail: sidsnet@sids-network.org
P.O. Box 520
Ledyard, Connecticut 06339
A charitable, non-profit volunteer agency, the SIDS Network is dedicated to eliminating Sudden Infant Death Syndrome through support of SIDS research, providing help for those who have been touched by SIDS and raising public awareness of SIDS through education. Services offered by the SIDS Network include peer counseling, monthly support meetings, crisis intervention counseling, referrals to other agencies, publications, a newsletter and educational literature and information for community service personnel.

SUICIDE

Suicide is one of the leading killers among young people today. The following Web sites and groups provide information and support to parents, family and friends who have lost a loved one to suicide. Many groups also provide resources and help to depressed people who feel they have nowhere to turn and are considering suicide.

American Foundation for Suicide Prevention

http://www.afsp.org
Email: inquiry@afsp.org
120 Wall Street, 22nd Floor
New York, New York 10005
Telephone: (888) 333-AFSP or (212) 363-3500
Fax: (212) 363-6237
Formed by business and community leaders and survivors of suicide in 1986, the American Foundation for Suicide Prevention supports research that furthers the understanding and treatment of depression and the prevention of suicide, provides information and education, promotes professional education for the recognition and treatment of depressed and suicidal individuals and supports programs for the survivors of suicide.

Metanoia

http://www.metanoia.org
Metanoia means "a change of mind." Metanoia encourages people to turn around, to face the light and leave the shadows behind them. Their mission is to dissolve the barriers that separate people who need help from the caregivers who can provide it. Through their Web site, you can talk on-line to a therapist, learn about Internet therapy, read the article "Choose a Competent Therapist" and a lengthy document on suicide

which, though geared toward persons contemplating suicide, also provides information to loved ones including what you can do to help a person who may be suicidal. The site also has an extensive list of links to suicide and depression resources and mental health providers and associations.

The National Mental Health Association
http://www.nmha.org
102 Prince Street
Alexandria, Virginia 22314-2971
Toll-free telephone: (800) 969-6642
Telephone: (703) 684-7722
Fax: (703) 684-5968
Dedicated to improving the mental health of all people and achieving victory over mental illness, the National Mental Health Association (NMHA) works to achieve its goals through advocacy, education, research and service. NMHA was at the forefront of efforts that resulted in the 1996 Mental Health Parity Act, which bars insurance companies from placing limits on mental health coverage, and their National Public Education Campaign on Clinical Depression, begun in 1993, continues to inform Americans on the symptoms of depression and provide information about treatment. Their newsletter and other publications are available on-line.

Suicide Prevention Advocacy Network (SPAN)
http://www.spanusa.org
5034 Odin's Way
Marietta, Georgia 30068
Toll-free telephone: (888) 649-1366
Fax: (770) 642-1419
A national, grassroots non-profit organization, SPAN was founded by a father who lost his adult daughter to suicide.

SPAN's goal is to create a comprehensive national suicide prevention effort by bridging the gap between various groups working to prevent suicide. SPAN generates advocacy letters to legislators, promotes education and awareness of suicide and petitions the U.S. government to declare suicide a national problem to develop an effective suicide prevention strategy and to require equality for mental health care.

Survivors of Loved Ones' Suicides (SOLOS)
http://www.1000deaths.com
E-mail: solos@1000deaths.com
This Web site, for the families and friends left behind when loved ones take their own lives, has E-mail support groups, on-line chats, memorials, information and statistics and resources. Their goals are to help those grieving after a loved one's suicide and to support survivors through advocacy efforts and charitable contributions to prevent suicide.

Survivors of Suicide
http://www.thewebpager.com/sos/
The Survivors of Suicide (SOS) Web site is dedicated to helping those who have lost loved ones to suicide by offering information and a safe place for survivors to share their struggles and pain and also to receive the comfort and understanding of others who have experienced similar losses. SOS offers on-line chats, members' stories, facts about suicide and memorials.

Appendix B

Memorial Web Pages

Many of the parents who contributed their stories to *Childlight* have set up Web sites to memorialize the children they have lost. Along with the stories of their children, some of the Web sites have links to other memorial Web pages and helpful resources for those dealing with losses of their own.

Chapter 2
Justin Harrison:
http://www.geocities.com/Heartland/Woods/6367/

Jessica Reed:
http://www.geocities.com/Heartland/Prairie/8216/

Chapter 3
Tobin MacDonald:
http://members.aol.com/MACBUFFET/index.html

Christopher Faller:
http://members.execulink.com/~bapar/memorial/member
/maria/index.htm

Chapter 4
Gerald LeMaster:
http://hometown.aol.com/mysugama/myhomepage/
memorial.html

Anthony Victor DeGennaro:
http://www.angelfire.com/oh/mdege

Chapter 5
Mike Robert Tiedt:
http://www.csidesign.com/miketribute/

Shane Hebert:
http://www.angelfire.com/la2/ShanesMom/index.html

Joshua Hedglin:
http://www.geocities.com/Heartland/Estates/4684

Brian Hotchkiss:
http://www.geocities.com/Heartland/Park/4746/brian.html

Lisa Flores:
www.geocities.com/bginlisa/loved.html

Chapter 6
Wendy Lynn Sunderlin:
http://www.angelfire.com/oh/wls19/index.html

Kevin "Ski" Lovenduski:
http://www.geocities.com/Heartland/Grove/3917/

Shari Stroyan:
http://members.tripod.com/~dsf_13/index.html

Chapter 7
Kevin Thomas Bowles:
www.VirtualMemorials.com

Chapter 8
Keith David Stenrose:
http://www.fortunecity.com/millennium/river/551/

Jeremy Tabler:
http://www.angelfire.com/ut/lovinangels/index.html

Joanna Bruner:
http://www.geocities.com/babbiejjb

Amanda Harris:
http://www.our-sma-angels.com/Amanda

Dylon Velard:
http://www.valinet.com/~kevlynn/

Casey Russell:
http://members.aol.com/FCR10/index.html

Nicholas Rosecrans:
http://www.geocities.com/Heartland/Pointe/5324

Chapter 10
Justin Daniels:
http://members.aol.com/angelj0830/

Appendix C

Tell Us Your Story

Do you have an after death contact story you would like to share? If so, please contact Dary Matera, preferably by E-mail, at:

Dary Matera
1628 S. Villas Lane
Chandler, AZ 85248-1804
E-mail: dary@goodnet.com OR dary@darymatera.com
Web site: www.darymatera.com

Please designate the category of After Death Contact, or ADC, in your correspondence.

Childlight 2 – Stories of parent/children ADCs.

Parentlight – Children/parent ADCs.

Siblinglight – Brother/sister ADCs

Friendlight – Friend ADCs

Spouselight – Spouse ADCs

Relativelight – Any other relative ADCs

Petlight – Pet ADCs

Miscellaneous – For ADC stories that don't fit in any of the above